EPIC Encounter

Experiencing Your Personal Identity and Freedom in Christ

Dave Park, D.D. & The Infusion Team

His Passion Publishing

Infusion Ministries

2021

We highly recommend you watch the free videos, which accompany this material.
You can find them on our website at infusionnow.org.

Graphics and Cover Design by Meghan Hamby
Layout/Design and edited by Kristie Kroschel and the Infusion staff.

Infusion Ministries is a national and international, interdenominational organization based in Knoxville, Tennessee. The purpose of Infusion Ministries is to awaken identity and establish freedom in the body of Christ. Our staff provides training and counseling through seminars, conferences, workshops, and resources with an emphasis on equipping pastors and small group leaders to do the same. We hope and pray that we will have the privilege to serve you and conduct one of our life-changing conferences or seminars for your group. Infusion Ministries is not a long-term counseling center. Through biblical truths and resources, we encourage and help believers in their walk with God.

Infusion Ministries
P.O.Box 22087
Knoxville, TN 37933
865-966-1153

infusionnow.org

WELCOME!

Welcome to Infusion Ministries EPIC Encounter training. The purpose of Infusion Ministries is to awaken identity and establish freedom in the body of Christ. Our deep desire is that you will have an EPIC experience with Jesus. We hope that His Word will come alive to you like never before and that you will personally hear His voice. It's our prayer that your encounter with God will not only lead you to a greater understanding of who you are in Christ, but also help you experience greater victory and personal freedom in your life. The contents of this training come from three key resources: *Stomping Out the Darkness, The Bondage Breaker – Youth Edition,* and *Free,* all of which I co-authored with Dr. Neil T. Anderson. The book *Free* is a forty-day devotional and a great follow-up to this training.

This workbook is meant to be used with the *EPIC Identity, Freedom, and The Lord's Prayer Journey* teaching videos found at our website: www.infusionnow.org/english-videos

Begin with **EPIC Identity**. Knowing who you are in Christ is the foundation of lasting spiritual freedom and an abundant life in Him.

After completing EPIC Identity, the next step in this three-part series is **EPIC Freedom.** You will learn to walk in the freedom you have in Him - freedom <u>from</u> spiritual strongholds and persistent sin patterns, and freedom <u>to</u> hear God's voice and do his will.

Once you have internalized EPIC Identity and after completing EPIC Freedom, the next step in this Encounter is the **EPIC Journey**. In this Holy Spirit-guided prayer experience, based upon the Lord's Prayer (Matthew 6:9-13), you will overcome spiritual conflicts and claim your identity and freedom in Christ.

Please visit infusionnow.org to find resources for almost every aspect of Christian living and ministry for both youth and adults. You can order online or call our office at (865) 966-1153 for assistance. If we can serve you in any way, please let us know.

Blessings,
Dr. Dave Park

FORWARD

I am on an amazing EPIC journey with the Lord. For the past 30+ years, God has had me studying through His Word and reading many Christian writers to understand everything I can about our identity as children of God and walking free from destructive habits and strongholds in our lives. It has been an intensely personal time, at times, too personal. My motivation was to learn more about these truths so I could help others with their issues, to help them walk free. But the Lord has, with dogged determination, brought these incredible truths back to my heart again and again to mend and repair my own soul and renew my mind and spirit. It is with a humble heart that I prepare these studies because I don't at all feel as though I am at the end of my journey. The truths that I'm going to be sharing with you I don't feel God gave to me because I am more committed, knowledgeable, or spiritually mature than others. I simply believe that the Lord must have felt that I personally need these truths more than others. I have never written anything that meant more to me personally than the messages in this study. I have had some great mentors to whom I am eternally thankful and you will certainly see their thumbprint on my life and work: Mark Bailey, Josh D. McDowell, and Neil T. Anderson. I am so grateful for these men and their teaching and discipleship. You have all helped me discover the truth of God's Word and those truths have set me free. Most of these notes, however, come directly from Neil Anderson's personal investment into my life and our books together. Neil, I carry the torch you so graciously gave me.

Over thirty years ago I said, "I do," to the girl of my dreams and each time we approach our anniversary, I realize with fresh eyes just how much God has transformed my life. My wife, Grace, has been my greatest mentor of all!

Galatians 5:13 reminds us, "for you were called to Freedom." Because of Jesus' loving work on the cross nothing can hold us captive; nothing can keep us in slavery without our consent. Don't give the world, the flesh or the devil permission to keep you in bondage another day. I pray as you go through this EPIC study that God's Word and Spirit pries open every prison gate, and you experience His great passion and freedom. God wants you to have an EPIC life; He paid for it, so come claim it!

Dr. Dave Park is the founder and president of Infusion Ministries and His Passion Ministries and lives in Knoxville, TN. Dave is a much sought-after speaker and counselor and is an international best-selling author. He has authored and co-authored many resources and books with Dr. Neil T. Anderson for youth and adults including *Stomping Out The Darkness and The Bondage Breaker—Youth Edition.* Dave's work has been nominated for three Gold Medallion awards.

CONTENTS

I am a child of God. John 1:12

I am Jesus' chosen friend. John 15:15

I am salt and light for everyone around me. Matt. 5:13,14

I am holy and accepted by God (justified). Rom. 5:1

I have been brought back (redeemed) and forgiven of all my sins. Col. 1:14

I am sure that the good work that God has started in me will be finished. Phil. 1:6

I can find grace and mercy in times of need. Heb. 4:16

I am sure that the good work that God has started in me will be finished. Phil. 1:6

I have been bought with a price. I belong to God. 1 Cor. 6:19,20

I have been adopted as God's child. Eph. 1:5

I am free from any condemning charges against me. Rom. 8:31

I am united to the Lord and am one in spirit with Him. 1 Cor. 6:17

I am a citizen of heaven with the rest of God's family. Eph. 2:19

I am born of God and the evil one cannot touch me. 1 John 5:18

I am a temple where the Holy Spirit lives. 1 Cor. 3:16; 1 Cor. 6:19

I am free forever from punishment. Rom. 8:1,2

I am sure all things work together for good. Rom. 8:28

I am a part of Christ's Body, part of His family. 1 Cor. 12:27

I am a saint, a holy one. Eph. 1:1

I am born of God and the evil one cannot touch me. 1 John 5:18

I am at peace with God and He has given me the work of making peace between Himself and other people. 2 Cor. 5:17

I am God's co-worker. 2 Cor. 6:1

I am God's building project. His handiwork created to do His work. Eph. 2:10

I am part of the true vine, joined to Christ and able to produce lots of fruit. John 15:1,5

I am seated with Christ in heaven. Eph. 2:6

I am able to do all things through Christ who gives me strength. Phil. 4:13

I am handpicked by Jesus to bear fruit. John 15:16

I cannot be separated from the love of God. Rom. 8:35

I am hidden with Christ in God. Col. 3:3

I am complete in Christ. Col. 2:10

I am a Spirit-empowered witness of Christ. Acts 1:8

EPIC

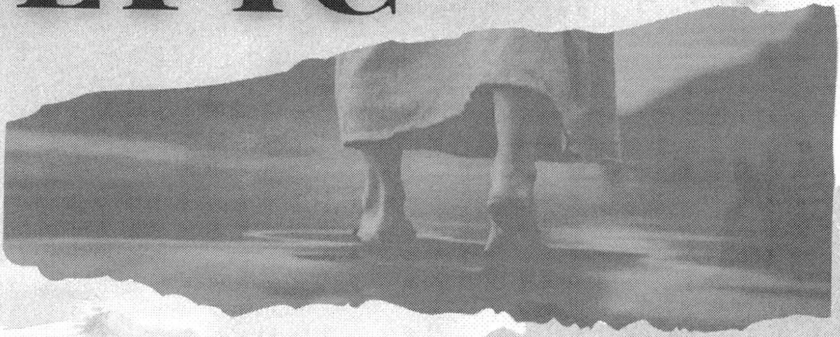

Identity

Authority is the right to rule. (Exousia)

Authority is the right to give commands, enforce obedience, take action, or make a final decision.

Authority is delegated from a higher power.

Power is the ability to rule. (Dunamis)

Power is the capacity to act. The power to do, to enforce what is desired.

Power should act under the submission (hupotasso) to those in authority.

Key Illustration: Police officer

Authority and power are given to the Apostles.

"And he called the twelve together and gave them power and authority over all demons and to cure diseases, and he sent them out to proclaim the kingdom of God and to heal" (Luke 9:1-2).

However, authority is not just an apostolic gift.

Authority and power are given to the Disciples.

"After this the Lord appointed seventy-two others and sent them on ahead of him, two by two, into every town and place where he himself was about to go" (Luke 10:1).

"The seventy–two returned with joy saying, 'Lord, even the demons are subject to us in Your name'" (Luke10:17).

"And he said to them, 'I saw Satan fall like lightning from heaven. Behold, I have given you authority to tread on serpents and scorpions, and over all the power of the enemy, and nothing shall hurt you'" (Luke 10:18-19).

Authority and power are given to the Church.

We share in Christ's authority. How do we know that we share in Christ's authority today?

Check out Ephesians 1:18-22: *"having the eyes of your hearts enlightened, that you may know what is the hope to which he has called you, what are the riches of his glorious inheritance in the saints, and what is the immeasurable greatness of his power toward us who believe, according to the working of his great might that he worked in Christ when he raised him from the dead and seated him at his right hand in the heavenly places, far above all rule and authority and power and dominion, and above every name that is named, not only in this age but also in the one to come. And he put all things under his feet and gave him as head over all things to the church…"*

Rejoice in your position in Christ, not in your authority or power.

"Nevertheless do not rejoice in this, that the spirits are subject to you, but rejoice that your names are written in heaven" (Luke 10:20).

Rejoice that you are a child of God and a saint, not in the power and authority you have in Him. Your position in Christ is more important than your authority and power in Christ.

The Authority of Christ

Jesus has all authority, not only in heaven but on earth as well! It was given to Him by the Father. Matthew 28:18 says, *"And Jesus came and said to them, 'All authority in heaven and on earth has been given to me.'"*

Jesus was given all authority as a result of His victory over sin and death. His resurrection validated His claim to have all authority (Ephesians 1:18-21).

Jesus' authority extends over everyone and everything for all time. (Ephesians 1:20-21, 1 Corinthians 15:24-28).

Our Authority in Christ

The right hand of God is identified as the place of all authority (Ephesians 1:20, 21).

Jesus is seated at God's right hand. Hebrews 1:3 says, *"He is the radiance of the glory of God and the exact imprint of his nature, and he upholds the universe by the word of his power. After making purification for sins, he sat down at the right hand of the Majesty on high,"*

We have been raised up with Christ and are now seated with Him at the right hand of God. Ephesians 2:4-6 says, *"But God, being rich in mercy, because of the great love with which he loved us, even when we were dead in our trespasses, made us alive together with Christ—by grace you have been saved— and raised us up with him and seated us with him in the heavenly places in Christ Jesus…,"*

We now share Christ's seat of authority!

Therefore, as we come under the authority of Christ, the devil must leave us alone when we stand firm and resist him. James 4:7 says, *"Submit yourselves therefore to God. Resist the devil, and he will flee from you."*

What was God thinking? When we think of the incredible authority that we have been given in Christ, we should be amazed that God chooses to share it with us! But He has done just that. Why? Because God has decided to use the body of Christ, the Church, and every Christian to be a living example of His great love, mercy, grace, and wisdom.

Ephesians 3:9-11 says, *"…and to bring to light for everyone what is the plan of the mystery hidden for ages in God, who created all things, so that through the church the manifold wisdom of God might now be made known to the rulers and authorities in the heavenly places. This was according to the eternal purpose that he has realized in Christ Jesus our Lord."*

Jesus proved that He had authority that came right from God the Father (Matthew 28:18, Hebrews 8:1), and He demonstrated His power and authority at the resurrection (Ephesians 1:19-23). The Apostle Paul uses four key words to describe Christ's awesome authority:

Exceeding greatness of God's **power** *(dunameos)*   Of the **strength** *(kratous)*
According to the **working** *(energian)*   Of His **might** *(ischuos)*

❖ Declaration against the enemy (out loud) ❖

By the power and the blood of the Lord Jesus Christ, I command, I don't suggest, I command any and all evil trying to influence me, my mind, or my body, to leave my presence. I am a child of the Most High God and my mind is my own, a quiet place for just me and God. I am free to hear the voice of God and pray as Jesus commanded us to pray.

❖ Prayer of Submission to God (out loud) ❖

Dear Heavenly Father, I know that You are here and present in my life and that You alone are all-powerful and mighty. I draw near to You and ask that You would draw near to me. I ask You to speak to me; I don't want to hear the words of man, I want to hear from You. Show me how to walk free today. In Jesus' name I pray, Amen.

"From now on, therefore, we regard no one according to the flesh. Even though we once regarded Christ according to the flesh, we regard him thus no longer. Therefore, if anyone is in Christ, he is a new creation. The old has passed away; behold, the new has come" (2 Corinthians 5:16-17).

Who are you?

At first, that might seem like a simple, even effortless question to answer; however, the way you answer that question reveals what you believe about the gospel and your spiritual birthright.

As Christians, we must realize why our needs for identity, acceptance, security, and significance cannot be fully met through appearance, performance, and social status. In this message, you will discover how your needs are met by becoming a child of God, and you will have a deeper understanding of the whole gospel and what it means to be a new creation in Christ.

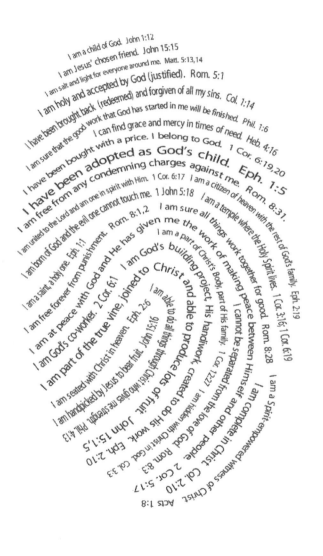

I am a child of God. John 1:12
I am Jesus' chosen friend. John 15:15
I am salt and light for everyone around me. Matt. 5:13,14
I am holy and accepted by God (justified). Rom. 5:1
I have been brought back (redeemed) and forgiven of all my sins. Col. 1:14
I am sure that the good work that God has started in me will be finished. Phil. 1:6
I can find grace and mercy in times of need. Heb. 4:16
I am sure I have been bought with a price. I belong to God. 1 Cor. 6:19,20
I have been adopted as God's child. Eph. 1:5
I am free from any condemning charges against me. Rom. 8:31
I am united to the Lord and am one in spirit with Him. 1 Cor. 6:17 I am a citizen of heaven with the rest of God's family. Eph. 2:19
I am born of God and the evil one cannot touch me. 1 John 5:18 I am a temple where the Holy Spirit lives. 1 Cor. 3:16; 1 Cor. 6:19
I am a saint, a holy one. Eph. 1:1 I am sure all things work together for good. Rom. 8:28
I am free forever from punishment. Rom. 8:1,2 I am a part of Christ's Body, part of His family. 1 Cor. 12:27
I am at peace with God and He has given me the work of making peace between Himself and other people. 2 Cor. 5:17
I am God's co-worker. 2 Cor. 6:1 I am God's building project. His handiwork created to do His work. Eph. 2:10
I am part of the true vine, joined to Christ and able to produce lots of fruit. John 15:1,5
I am seated with Christ in heaven. Eph. 2:6 I am able to do all things through Christ who gives me strength. Phil. 4:13
I am handpicked by Jesus to bear fruit. John 15:16 I cannot be separated from the love of God. Rom. 8:3
I am complete in Christ. Col. 2:10 I am hidden with Christ in God. Col. 3:3
I am a Spirit-empowered witness of Christ. Acts 1:8

"Identity In Christ" means knowing and believing what God says about me.

True about me before Christ	True about me in Christ
I was a sinner (Romans 3:23, Romans 5:8)	I am a saint, a holy one (Philippians 1:1, Ephesians 1:1 Colossians 1:2, 1 Corinthians 1:2)
I was lost (Luke 19:10)	I am found (Luke 15:6,9,24)
I was a stranger (Ephesians 2:19)	I am a citizen (Ephesians 2:19)
I was dead (Ephesians 2:1-3)	I am alive (Ephesians 2:4-7)
I was an orphan (John 14:18)	I am adopted (Ephesians 1:5, Romans 8:15)
I was guilty (James 2:10)	I am forgiven (Ephesians 1:7)

Christ supplies my every need

In Christ We Experience	Without Christ We Experience
Acceptance (Romans 5:1, 8,15,17)	Rejection (Ephesians 2:1-3)
Belonging (1 Corinthians 6:17)	Alienation (Ephesiand 4:18 KJV)
Purpose (2 Corinthians 5:17-18, Colossians 3:4)	Meaninglessness (Ecclesiastes 1:2)
Power (Philippians 4:13)	Weakness (Psalm 27:1)
Authority (Acts 1:8)	Timidity (2 Timothy 1:7)
Submission (Romans 13:1-2)	Rebellion (1 Timothy 1:9)
Provision (Philippians 4:19)	Worry (1 Peter 5:7)
Guidance (Romans 8:14)	Being Lost (Hebrews 5:11-14)
Security (Romans 8:31)	Fear (2 Timothy 1:7, Matthew10:26-33)
Significance (John 15:1,5)	Inferiority (Romans 8:37)
Peace (Galatians 5:22)	Confusion (1 Corinthians 14:33)
Freedom (Galatians 5:1)	Bondage (1 John 4:4)

False Identity Equations

"Thus says the LORD 'Let not a wise man boast of his wisdom, let not the mighty man boast of his might, let not a rich man boast of his riches, but let him who boasts boast in this, that he understands and knows Me, that I am the LORD who practices steadfast love, justice, and righteousness in the earth. For in these things I delight,' declares the LORD" (Jeremiah 9:23-24).

We must understand our true identity in Christ and realize our true spiritual heritage and birthright as a child of the Most High God. This means letting the Lord break down the false identity equations that have been constructed by the world, the flesh, and the devil and replacing them with the only identity equation that works:

> ## You + Christ = Wholeness and Meaning
> ## Intimacy with God = Love, Peace and Completeness

False identity equations are formulas that are developed apart from who we are in Christ to bolster and augment our false sense of being. We all want to belong and have a sense of significance. In fact, those are legitimate needs. The problem comes when we try to meet them apart from who we really are in Christ.

For example:

> ### Lies of the World
>
> - The correct look + the precise form = true beauty
> - Appearance + admiration = belonging
> - Respect + approval = fitting in or leadership
> - Performance + accomplishment = significance
> - The right act + the proper presentation = importance
> - Status + recognition = safety and security
> - Identification with the right group + standing = protection and acceptance

Why does a physically beautiful girl struggle with anorexia or bulimia? There's a false identity equation deeply rooted in her mind. The lie demands that she find the correct look and precise form to achieve true beauty. The problem is that the form and look never come. The enemy is good at blinding eyes to the truth.

Why does a bright young man join a gang? There's a false identity equation deeply rooted in his mind. The lie insists that he identify with the right group and that he achieve standing and position. But a criminal record, a poor paying job, and some battle scars are all that come with the deal; that is if he isn't killed.

The same false identity equation can lead a man to spend money he really can't afford to join the golf club and hours at lessons when he really needs and wants to be home. Satan loves to mold our fragile egos with any false identity equation he can. If one equation doesn't work, he is happy to introduce another.

The only thing that protects us is knowing the truth, and the only identity equation that works is:

You + Christ = Wholeness and Meaning

False identity equations are not cute or something that people will just grow out of. They are not just a phase; they are controlling and deadly. In one Infusion Ministries survey of over 1,100 Christian youth, we found that:

22% said, "I have deprived myself of food to gain a more attractive body."

19% said, "I wish I were someone else."

19% said, "I have felt compelled to cut myself."

16% said, "I have cut myself and left scars."

13% said, "I have purged or made myself throw up."

5% said, "I have taken diet pills on a regular basis."

Your identity as a believer does not come from your outward appearance, performance, or social status.

Your identity comes from being a child of God. Your sense of worth comes not from self but from being created in the image of God. When we come to realize that Christ is in us, and we are in Christ, we won't worry about our self-image anymore.

ORIGINAL CREATION

Genesis 1,2

PHYSICAL LIFE
*United with
inner self*

SPIRITUAL LIFE
Inner self united with God

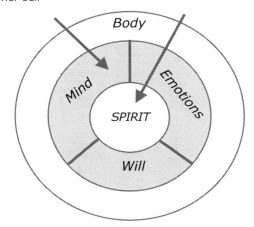

SIGNIFICANCE:

Man had a divine purpose (Genesis 1:28)

SAFETY AND SECURITY:

All of man's needs were provided for (Genesis 1:29)

BELONGING:

Man had a sense of belonging (Genesis 2:18)

*Figure 1A: pg. 12 from Stomping Out the Darkness
by Neil Anderson & Dave Park
Figure 1A pg. 12*

Created in the Image of God

Each of us has worn a mask or misrepresented ourselves at one time or another—probably because we've felt the pain of rejection, guilt, shame or insecurity, and insignificance. Although we now struggle for acceptance, security, and significance, this is not how God created us to live in the beginning. Both Adam and Eve were created in the image of God (Genesis 1:26-27).

"then the LORD God formed the man of the dust from the ground and breathed into his nostrils the breath of life, and the man became a living creature" (Genesis 2:7).

Adam and Eve were alive in two ways.

First, they were physically alive (Bios). The soul/spirit is in union with the body. To die physically is the separation of the soul/spirit from the body.

Secondly, they were spiritually alive (Zoë).
Their soul/spirit was in union with God. To be spiritually dead is to be separated from God (Ephesians 2:1). For the Christian, to be spiritually alive is to be "in Christ" or to be "a child of God, born again" (spiritually). Because Adam and Eve were connected to God, they had a deep sense of purpose and meaning in life.

EFFECTS OF THE FALL

Genesis 3:8–4:9

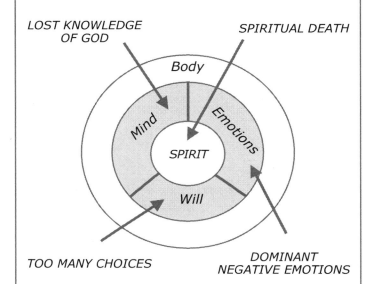

LOST KNOWLEDGE OF GOD

SPIRITUAL DEATH

TOO MANY CHOICES

DOMINANT NEGATIVE EMOTIONS

REJECTED:

Therefore a need to belong

WEAK AND HELPLESS:

Therefore a need of strength and self-control

GUILT AND SHAME:

Therefore a need for self-worth

*Figure 1B: pg. 16 from *Stomping Out the Darkness*
by Neil Anderson & Dave Park

The Effects of the Fall

What Adam and Eve immediately lost was spiritual life, not physical life. Their spiritual life had been characterized by the vital relationship of dependence on God. Adam's sin was deliberately breaking God's command. It resulted in the loss of his intimate relationship with God.

- You will surely die (Genesis 2:17).

- You were dead in your trespasses and sins (Ephesians 2:1).

- Sin entered the world through one man, and death entered through sin (Romans 5:12).

1. Spiritual Death (Spirit)

While Adam and Eve didn't die physically right away, they did die spiritually (Genesis 2:16-17). As a consequence, every descendant of Adam is born into the world physically alive but spiritually dead (Romans 5:12, 1 Corinthians 15:21-22).

2. Lost knowledge of God (Mind)

It became painfully clear that Adam and Eve had lost their intimacy and what they knew about God as they attempted to hide from an all-knowing and omnipresent God (Genesis 3:7-8). Before accepting Christ, we are darkened in our understanding of God because we do not have the life of Christ in us (Ephesians 4:18). Paul said that the natural or unsaved person, who is spiritually dead, cannot discern the things of God because such things are not understood through the flesh, but only through the Spirit (1 Corinthians 2:14). In this condition, we can know things about God, but we can't really know Him in an intimate and personal way. That is not possible until we establish a relationship with Him through His Son Jesus Christ.

3. Too many choices (Will)

They felt depressed and angry. Before the fall, Adam and Eve had only one bad choice that they could make—to eat from the forbidden tree; other than that, they could make no bad choices. After the fall, they were slammed with choices, both good and bad. Overwhelmed, they became depressed and angry. Today depression is the 'common cold' of mental illness. Despite new drugs and medical advances, more people are experiencing depression than ever before.
(A helpful resource: *Stomping Out Depression* by Neil Anderson and Dave Park.)

4. Negative Feelings (Emotions)

They felt fear and anxiety. The first emotion recorded after the fall of mankind was fear (Genesis 3:10). Today, anxiety disorders are the number one mental health problem in the world.
(A helpful resource: *Stomping Out Fear* by Neil Anderson and Dave Park.)

> They felt guilt and shame: therefore, a need for self-worth.
> They felt weak and helpless: therefore, a need for strength and self-control.
> They felt rejected: therefore, a need to belong.

It is sin when we attempt to meet our basic needs apart from Christ; to live independently of God. However, God promises to meet all our needs as we live our life "in Christ."

EPIC CHALLENGE

1. How much of your identity and sense of worth comes from what you do?

2. According to the Bible, what is your true identity based on?

3. Why do you think we often struggle with guilt and shame?

4. How does Christ help us feel safe and secure?

5. In what four ways did Adam and Eve's sin, or the fall, affect us and all mankind?

6. What is a false identity equation?

7. Ask the Lord to show you what your false identity equations are. Write down any He reveals or you see in your life.

8. What is the only identity equation that really works?

9. What is the most important truth you learned from this message?

1. The Last Adam (Jesus Christ)

Jesus was like Adam before the fall; He was both physically and spiritually alive because He was conceived by the Spirit and born of a virgin. Unlike Adam, Jesus never sinned. He modeled perfectly for us how to live free in a fallen world but was completely dependent on God the Father. Jesus was far more than just a model; He is the only giver of life and freedom. It is His passion to give eternal life to all who turn to Him. He said, *"...I came that they may have life, and have it abundantly"* (John 10:10).

2. Life is Recovered "In Christ"

The Bible tells us *"for me to live is Christ"* (Philippians 1:21). Therefore, *"life"* is recovered in Christ. *"Whoever has the Son has life; whoever does not have the Son of God does not have life"* (1 John 5:12).

3. Life Determines Identity

A Christian is not simply a person who gets forgiven, gets to go to heaven, gets the Holy Spirit, and who gets a new nature. A Christian, in terms of their deepest identity, is a saint, a child of God, deeply loved by Him.

> Being a Christian is not just about getting something; it is about being someone.
>
> The point is not what you have, but who you are.
>
> It is not what you do that determines who you are;
> it is who you are that determines what you do.

Jesus Came to Give Us an EPIC Life

The difference between good works and identity in Christ is the difference between light and life. Life determines identity; good works determine light. The gospel of John puts it this way, *"In him was life, and the life was the light of men"* (John 1:4). Notice that light does not produce life. Rather spiritual life is the light of the world. Good works can not produce life, but life always produces good works. Jesus did not come to earth to compel us to do good works but, rather, to receive Him as the only source of eternal life. Jesus said, *"I am the resurrection and the life. Whoever believes in me, though he die, yet shall he live"* (John 11:25).

"But you are a chosen race, a royal priesthood, a holy nation, a people for his own possession, that you may proclaim the excellencies of him who called you out of darkness into his marvelous light. Once you were not a people, but now you are God's people; once you had not received mercy, but now you have received mercy" (1 Peter 2:9-10).

If you wanted to save a dead man, you would have to do two things:

First, cure the disease that caused him to die.
Jesus died for our sins and extends His forgiveness to all who will receive it (Romans 3:23, Ephesians 1:7).

Second, give him life.
In Christ, we have a new life (John 5:24).

Justification is more than, "Just as if I had never sinned!" When Jesus justified us, He took away all our sin. But He also gave us new life and holiness.

Eternal life is not something you get when you die (1 John 5:12). The moment we received Christ, we received eternal life and became a child of God (John 1:12).

In Christ, we now have *life, acceptance, security, and significance*. It's all restored in Christ!

Your Invitation to Life

Jesus said, *"I came that they may have life, and have it abundantly"* (John 10:10).

Have you discovered the joy and peace of personally accepting Jesus' invitation to life? Perhaps you have believed in the existence of God and His Son and have tried to live a good life, but have never consciously invited Him to be your Savior and Lord.

No matter who you are or what you have done, at this very moment, you can make the decision of a lifetime. Right now, Jesus is knocking at the door of your heart. He offers you the same life-change which millions through the centuries have received with wonderful results. He has already paid the penalty for your sin. He is asking you, in the quietness of your heart, to put your trust in Him.

Here are four spiritual truths that will help you discover how to know God personally and experience the full and abundant life He promises.

1. God loves you and wants to have a personal relationship with you.

"For God so loved the world, that he gave his only Son, that whoever believes in him should not perish but have eternal life" (John 3:16).

"This is eternal life, that they may know you, the only true God and Jesus Christ whom you have sent" (John 17:3).

Why is it that most people are not experiencing a life of freedom and the abundant life? Because...

2. Our sin cuts us off from God so we cannot have a personal relationship with Him and experience His love.

We Have All Sinned

"For all have sinned and fall short of the glory of God" (Romans 3:23).

We were all created to have a personal relationship with God. Because we all chose to go our own independent way, our relationship with God was broken. The fact that we are selfish and self-centered is obvious because we either rebel against God or do not care about Him. This evidence is what the Bible calls "sin."

We Were Cut Off From God

"For the wages of sin is death" [spiritual separation from God] (Romans 6:23).

This diagram illustrates that God is holy (pure and sinless), and we are sinful. A great gulf separates us from God. The arrows illustrate our attempts to reach God and the abundant life through our own efforts, such as a good life, philosophy, or religion—but we inevitably fail.

3. **Jesus Christ is God's only cure for our sin. Through Him, you can know and experience God's love.**

Jesus Died In Our Place

"but God demonstrates His love for us in that while we were still sinners, Christ died for us" (Romans 5:8).

Jesus Rose from the Dead

"that Christ died for our sins in accordance with the Scriptures, that he was buried, that he was raised on the third day in accordance with the Scriptures, and that he appeared to Peter, then to the twelve. Then he appeared to more than five hundred brothers at one time, most of whom are still alive, though some have fallen asleep" (1 Corinthians 15:3-6).

Jesus Is the Only Way to God

"Jesus said to him, 'I am the way, and the truth, and the life. No one comes to the Father except through me'" (John 14:6).

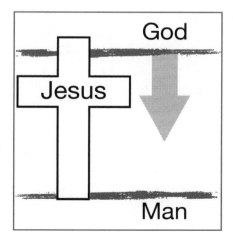

This diagram illustrates that God has bridged the gulf that separates us from Him by sending His Son, Jesus Christ, to die on the cross in our place to pay the penalty for our sins.

It is not enough just to know these truths!

4. We must individually receive Jesus Christ as Savior and Lord; then we can know and experience God's love and plan for our lives.

We Must Receive Christ

"But to all who did receive him, who believed in his name, he gave the right to become children of God" (John 1:12).

We Receive Christ Through Faith

"For by grace you have been saved through faith; and this is not of your own doing; it is the gift of God, not a result of works, so that no one may boast" (Ephesians 2:8-9).

When We Receive Christ, We Experience a New Birth

"Now there was a man of the Pharisees named Nicodemus, a ruler of the Jews. This man came to Jesus by night and said to him, 'Rabbi, we know that you are a teacher come from God, for no one can do these signs that you do unless God is with him.'

Jesus answered him, 'Truly, truly, I say to you, unless one is born again he cannot see the kingdom of God.'

Nicodemus said to him, 'How can a man be born when he is old? Can he enter a second time into his mother's womb and be born?'

Jesus answered, 'Truly, truly, I say to you, unless one is born of water and the Spirit, he cannot enter the kingdom of God. That which is born of the flesh is flesh, and that which is born of the Spirit is spirit. Do not marvel that I said to you, 'You must be born again.' The wind blows where it wishes, and you hear its sound, but you do not know where it comes from or where it goes. So it is with everyone who is born of the Spirit" (John 3:1-8).

Receiving Christ involves turning to God from self (repentance) and trusting Christ to come into our lives to forgive our sins and to make us what He wants us to be. To agree **intellectually** that Jesus Christ is the Son of God and that He died on the cross for our sins is not enough. Nor is it enough to have an **emotional** experience. We receive Jesus Christ by **faith** as an act of the **will**.

If you haven't received Christ, you can right now, by faith through prayer (prayer is talking with God). God knows your heart and is not as concerned with your words as He is with the attitude of your heart. The following is a suggested prayer:

Lord Jesus, I believe that You are the Son of God, and I want to know You personally. I confess that I need You. Thank You for dying on the cross for me and my sins. I open the door of my life and receive You as my Savior and Lord. I trust You now to forgive all my sins and to give me eternal life. Take control of my life. Make me the kind of person You want me to be. Thank You for saving me and making me Your child. Amen. ❖

(*Your Most Important Relationship,* San Bernardino, CA: jointly published by Campus Crusade for Christ International and Youth for Christ/USA, 1985, pp.1-11.)

If you prayed to receive Christ today, write your decision in the space below:

Eternal life doesn't start when you die; rather, it starts the moment you receive Christ as your Savior! God wants you to have an EPIC life, filled with His Presence. The enemy wants to steal your joy and security. Don't let him. Write down the important life–changing decision you made.

Today I accepted Christ as my personal Lord and Savior!

Signed:_____

Today's Date:_____

Augustine said, "You have made us for yourself, and our hearts are restless until they rest in *you.*"

Read Ephesians 2:12-13.

EPIC CHALLENGE

1. Read Romans 8:1. What does God say about our sin if we have put our trust in Christ as Savior?

2. Have you ever felt condemnation? Condemnation is a punishing thought, to show guilt, to declare unfit for use. What does Colossians 2:13-14 say about our sin?

3. You have been forgiven all your sins past, present, and future; the slate has been wiped clean. What does Hebrews 4:16 say we can now do?

4. What was your identity before salvation? Read Ephesians 2:11.

5. The Bible says that if you have trusted Christ for your salvation, that now you are a child of God. From these scriptures, identify the terms used to explain this transformation.

   John 3:6

   2 Corinthians 6:18

   Titus 3:5

   Galatians 3:26

   Ephesians 2:1-2

Something Old, Something New

What happened to you when you became a child of God through faith in Jesus? Did anything really change inside of you? Satan wants you to believe that you are the same messed-up piece of sinful humanity that you were before you trusted Christ. Is that true? NO WAY!

"...Remember that you were at that time separate from Christ, alienated from the commonwealth of Israel and strangers to the covenants of promise, having no hope and without God in the world. But now in Christ Jesus, you who once were far away have been brought near through the blood of Christ" (Ephesians 2:12-13).

You see, God sees you as you truly are—in Christ. That is your position—joined to Jesus Christ and united with His life. Even though you may not feel brand new, you are actually a whole new person inside. Unfortunately, most Christians don't realize this truth and so are perishing for lack of knowledge (Hosea 4:6).

Do you see yourself as a product of your past or as "sin" and "dead"? God wants us to begin to see ourselves as "alive" and "in Christ," as the "saints" we really are!

Over 170 times in the New Testament, Paul makes reference to the fact that we are now placed "in Him." Satan can whine and scream all he wants, but nothing can change the truth that you are now placed "in Christ."

You may see yourself as a weak, struggling Christian who just cannot seem to get it together. You must see yourself as God sees you. God sees you as His dear child, holy and blameless, with everything you need to walk in victory instead of failure! Who is right? God is! You see, deep down inside, the real you is in Christ! You are forgiven, free from sin's power, united to the One who has all power!

Believe it or Not!

"What shall we say then? Are we to continue in sin that grace may abound? By no means! How can we who died to sin still live in it? Do you not know that all of us who have been baptized into Christ Jesus were baptized into his death? We were buried therefore with him by baptism into death, in order that, just as Christ was raised from the dead by the glory of the Father, we too might walk in newness of life.

For if we have been united with him in a death like his, we shall certainly be united with him in a resurrection like his. We know that our old self was crucified with him in order that the body of sin might be brought to nothing, so that we would no longer be enslaved to sin. For one who has died has been set free from sin.

Now if we have died with Christ, we believe that we will also live with him. We know that Christ, being raised from the dead, will never die again; death no longer has dominion over him. For the death he died he died to sin, once for all, but the life he lives he lives to God.

So you also must consider yourselves dead to sin and alive to God in Christ Jesus. Let not sin therefore reign in your mortal body, to make you obey its passions" (Romans 6:1-12).

In the Bible when you find a:

Truth – Believe it!

Promise – Claim it!

Command – Obey it!

The Bible says we are already in Christ. It is true of us now whether we believe it or not! The Bible refers to our position in Christ in the past tense.

You cannot do for yourself what God has already done for you! For example, how can you die to sin? (Romans 6:2).

God says we have been joined to Christ in the following ways:

In His death   Romans 6:3, Galatians 2:20, Colossians 3:1-3

In His Burial   Romans 6:4

In His Resurrection   Romans 6:5,8,11

In His Life   Romans 5:10-11

In His Power   Ephesians 1:19-20

In His Inheritance   Romans 8:16-17, Ephesians 1:11-12

In His Ascension   Ephesians 2:6

Anderson, N. T., & Park, D. (2001). *The Bondage Breaker Youth Edition* (pp.52). Eugene OR: Harvest House Publishers.

Who Am I In Christ — I Am Accepted

John 1:12	I am a child of God.
John 15:15	I am Jesus' chosen friend.
Romans 5:1	I am holy and acceptable to God (justified).
1 Corinthians 3:16	I am united to the Lord and am one with Him in Spirit.
1 Corinthians 6:19-20	I have been bought with a price, I belong to God.
1 Corinthians 12:27	I am part of Christ's body, part of His family.
Ephesians 1:1	I am a saint, a holy one.
Ephesians 1:5	I have been adopted as God's child.
Colossians 1:14	I have been bought back (redeemed) and forgiven of all my sins.
Colossians 2:10	I am complete in Christ.

Who Am I In Christ — I Am Secure

Romans 8:1-2	I am forever free from punishment.
Romans 8:28	I am sure all things work together for good.
Romans 8:31	I am free of any condemning charges against me.
Romans 8:35	I cannot be separated from the love of God.
Colossians 3:3	I am hidden with Christ in God.
Philippians 1:6	I am sure the good work God has started in me will be finished.
Ephesians 2:19	I am a citizen of heaven with the rest of God's family.
1 John 5:18	I am born of God and the evil one cannot touch me.

Who Am I In Christ — I Am Significant

Matthew 5:13-14	I am salt and light for everyone around me.
John 15:1,5	I am part of the true vine, able to produce lots of fruit.
John15:16	I am hand-picked by Jesus to bear fruit.
Acts 1:8	I am a spirit-empowered witness for Christ.
1 Corinthians 3:16, 6:19	I am a temple where the Holy Spirit lives.
2 Corinthians 5:18	I am at peace with God and He has given me the work of making peace between Himself and other people.
2 Corinthians 6:1	I am God's co-worker.
Ephesians 2:6	I am seated with Christ in heaven.
Ephesians 2:10	I am God's building project, His handy-work, created to do His work.
Philippians 4:13	I am able to do all things through Christ who gives me strength.

Anderson, N. T., & Park, D. (2007). Who am I? In *Stomping out the Darkness* (pp. 26-28). Bloomington MN: Bethany House Publishers.

Hebrews 11:6   James 2:20   John 13:17

Believe ⟶ **Behave** ⟶ **Feel**

What you believe determines how you behave and how you behave determines how you feel.

> We must choose to believe that what God says about us is true.
>
> It remains true whether we **feel like** it's true or not.
>
> It remains true whether we **act like** it's true or not! (Romans 6:6-9)

The order of Scripture is first the **knowing** (cognitive), then **being** (affective), and finally **doing** (volitional). What we need to know first is the truth (John 8:32).

Very often, we feel powerless to resist temptation. So we wonder if we need some new experience with God or special blessing from Him in order to be victorious over sin. But God has already told us that we are dead to sin and that we can now say "no" to sin and "yes" to God!

In our zeal to correct our behavior, we often skip over the truth (doctrine of our identity in Christ) and the important process of internalizing truth (a deep sense of being in Christ) and jump right to the practical "how to's" of life. But if we ignore the biblical process of growth, we can easily fall into legalism or some form of Christian behavior modification. We must first establish a proper belief system based on the character of God and who we are in Christ. If what you believe does not reflect the truth, then what you feel does not reflect reality!

What we receive when we are in Christ:

Acceptance	Romans 5:1,8,15,17
Belonging	1 Corinthians 6:17
Purpose	2 Corinthians 5:17-18
Power	Philippians 4:13
Authority	Acts 1:8
Submission	Romans 13:1,2
Provision	Philippians 4:19
Guidance	Romans 8:14
Security	Romans 8:31
Significance	John 15:1,5
Peace	Galatians 5:22
Freedom	Galatians 5:1

I am a child of God. John 1:12
I am Jesus' chosen friend. John 15:15
I am salt and light for everyone around me. Matt. 5:13,14
I am holy and accepted by God (justified). Rom. 5:1
I have been brought back (redeemed) and forgiven of all my sins. Col. 1:14
I am sure that the good work that God has started in me will be finished. Phil. 1:6
I can find grace and mercy in times of need. Heb. 4:16
I have been bought with a price. I belong to God. 1 Cor. 6:19,20
I have been adopted as God's child. Eph. 1:5
I am free from any condemning charges against me. Rom. 8:31f.
I am united to the Lord and am one in spirit with Him. 1 Cor. 6:17
I am a citizen of heaven with the rest of God's family. Eph. 2:19
I am born of God and the evil one cannot touch me. 1 John 5:18
I am a temple where the Holy Spirit lives. 1 Cor. 3:16; 1 Cor. 6:19
I am a saint, a holy one. Eph. 1:1
I am sure all things work together for good. Rom. 8:28
I am free forever from punishment. Rom. 8:1,2
I am a part of Christ's Body, part of His family. 1 Cor. 12:27
I am at peace with God. 2 Cor. 6:1
I am God's co-worker. 2 Cor. 6:1
I am God's building project. His handiwork, created to do His work. Eph. 2:10
I am part of the true vine, joined to Christ and able to produce lots of fruit. John 15:1,5
I cannot be separated from the love of God. Rom. 8:35f.
I am seated with Christ in heaven. Eph. 2:6
I am able to do all things through Christ who gives me strength. Phil. 4:13
I am handpicked by Jesus to bear fruit. John 15:16
I am hidden with Christ in God. Col. 3:3
I am complete in Christ. Col. 2:10
I am a Spirit-empowered witness of Christ. Acts 1:8

EPIC CHALLENGE

1. What does Romans 6:11 say that our relationship to sin is now that we are in Christ?

2. Romans 6:23 tells us that the wages of sin is death, but what gift does God give us if we choose Christ as our Savior?

3. What does Romans 8:39 say can separate us from the love of God now that we are in Christ?

4. If you were to walk today "in Christ" rather than "in self" what would be different about your day?

5. What are the seven ways you have been joined to Christ? (See page 31 if you need help)

6. What happened to you when you became a child of God through faith in Christ? In what ways did God change you inside?

7. The order of Scripture is first <u>knowing</u>, then _____, and finally _____

What we need to know first is_____. John 8:32

"Jesus continued, 'There was a man who had two sons. The younger one said to his father, 'Father, give me my share of the estate,'" (Luke 15:11-12 NIV).

This son:

Acceptance	was loved and accepted unconditionally by the father
Belonging	was part of a family
Purpose	had a purpose in the family business
Power	had the right to govern the father's estate
Authority	had the right to do the father's business
Submission	could do the father's will
Provision	had good food and a warm home to sleep in
Guidance	had his father's guidance, wisdom, and direction
Security	didn't have to worry about the future, the father had plenty
Significance	was the father's son and a significant part of the family
Peace	could rest easy and live at peace in the father's care
Freedom	was free to do what he knew was right on the father's behalf

The son rejected the love of the father, believing the father was holding him back from real freedom. The son demanded his independence. So the father gave him his share of the property.

"Not long after that, the younger son got together all he had, set off for a distant country and there squandered his wealth in wild living. After he had spent everything, there was a severe famine in that whole country, and he began to be in need. So he went and hired himself out to a citizen of that country, who sent him to his fields to feed pigs. He longed to fill his stomach with the pods that the pigs were eating, but no one gave him anything" (Luke 15:13-16 NIV).

Rejecting his relationship with His Father, he now has forfeited the benefits of being in the Father's household.

The enemy comes to **steal**, **kill**, and **destroy**, and his strategy is always to move us away from the Father (John 10:10).

Finally, the son realized life without fellowship with the father was not good at all.

"When he came to his senses, he said, 'How many of my father's hired servants have food to spare, and here I am starving to death! I will set out and go back to my father and say to him: Father, I have sinned against heaven and against you. I am no longer worthy to be called your son; make me like one of your hired servants.' So he got up and went to his father" (Luke 15:17-20 NIV).

He rejected the Father and walked away. It is not until his life is in ruins that he begins to realize he has been deceived; he has made a terrible mistake.

- What was truly valuable has been **stolen**.

- The relationship and fellowship he must have to survive may be **dead**.

- His future may be **destroyed**.

But now, his only hope of life is found in the very one he has treated with such contempt. He is desperate... he simply has nowhere else to turn. Even though he cannot expect to belong again, to sleep in his own bed or to carry the family name, perhaps hard work can get him some small wage to make some semblance of a life.
So he makes his way back to his father's house.

"But while he was still a long way off, his father saw him and was filled with compassion for him; he ran to his son, threw his arms around him and kissed him" (Luke 15:20 NIV).

The son was no doubt shocked by this unexpected love and embrace. He then reminded his father of what he had done and what he was so heartsick about.

"The son said to him, 'Father, I have sinned against heaven and against you. I am no longer worthy to be called your son'" (Luke 15:21 NIV).

"But the father said to his servants, 'Quick! Bring the best robe and put it on him. Put a ring on his finger and sandals on his feet. Bring the fattened calf and kill it. Let's have a feast and celebrate. For this son of mine was dead and is alive again; he was lost and is found.' So they began to celebrate" (Luke 15:22-24 NIV).

There are four gifts the Father longs to give each of us as we humbly return to a life in right fellowship with Him, and all of them relate to who we are in Christ.

"For you did not received the spirit of slavery to fall back into fear, but you have received the Spirit of adoption as sons, by whom we cry out, 'Abba, Father!' The Spirit himself bears witness with our spirit that we are children of God" (Romans 8:15-16).

Four gifts the Father longs to give each who returns to right relationship with Him:

1. Quick! Bring the best **robe** and put it on him (Luke 15:22, Romans 4:7-8).

2. Put a **ring** on his finger (Luke 15:22).

3. Put **sandals** on his feet (Luke 15:22, Galatians 4:3-7).

4. Bring the fattened calf.... and **celebrate** (Luke 15:23).

Robe = Holiness & Righteousness   **Sandals** = Freedom

Ring = Authority   **Celebration** = Restored Fellowship

"In the same way we also, when we were children, were enslaved to the elementary principles of the world. But when the fullness of time had come, God sent forth his Son, born of woman, born under the law, to redeem those who were under the law, so that we might receive adoption as sons" (Galatians 4:3-5).

Who Am I In Christ

- I am the salt of the earth (Matthew 5:13).

- I am the light of the world (Matthew 5:14).

- I am a child of God (John 1:12).

- I am part of the vine, and Christ's life flows through me. (John 15:1,5).

- I am Christ's friend (John 15:5).

- I am chosen by Christ to bear fruit (John 15:16).

- I am Christ's personal witness sent out to tell everybody about Him (Acts 1:8).

- I am a slave to God, making me holy and giving me eternal life (Romans 6:22).

- I am a child of God; I can call Him my Father (Romans 8:14-15, Galatians 3:26, 4:6).

- I am a coheir with Christ, inheriting His glory (Romans 8:17).

- I am a temple—a dwelling place—for God. His Spirit and His life live in me (1 Corinthians 3:16, 6:19).

- I am joined forever to the Lord and am one spirit with Him (1 Corinthians 6:17).

- I am a part of Christ's Body (1 Corinthians 12:27).

- I am a new person. My past is forgiven and everything is new (2 Corinthians 5:17).

- I am at peace with God, and He has given me the work of helping others find peace with Him (2 Corinthians 5:18-19).

- I am a child of God and will receive the inheritance He has promised (Galatians 4:6-7).

- I am a saint, a holy person (Ephesians 1:1, Philippians 1:1, Colossians 1:2).

- I am a citizen of heaven seated in heaven right now (Ephesians 2:6, Philippians 3:20).

- I am God's building project, His handiwork, created in Christ to do His work (Ephesians 2:10).

- I am a citizen of heaven with all of God's family (Ephesians 2:19).

- I am a prisoner of Christ so I can help others (Ephesians 3:1; 4:1).

- I am righteous and holy (Ephesians 4:24).

- I am hidden with Christ in God (Colossians 3:3).

- I am an expression of the life of Christ because He is my life (Colossians 3:4).

- I am chosen of God, holy and dearly loved (Colossians 3:12, 1 Thessalonians 1:4).

- I am a child of light and not of darkness (1 Thessalonians 5:5).

- I am chosen to share in God's heavenly calling (Hebrews 3:1).

- I am part of Christ; I share in His life (Hebrews 3:14).

- I am one of God's living stones, being built up in Christ as a spiritual house (1 Peter 2:5).

- I am a member of a chosen race, a royal priesthood, a holy nation, a people belonging to God (1 Peter 2:9-10).

- I am only a visitor to this world in which I temporarily live (1 Peter 2:11).

- I am an enemy of the devil (1 Peter 5:8).

- I am a child of God, and I will be like Christ when He returns (1 John 3:1-2).

- I am born again in Christ, and the evil one—the devil—cannot touch me (1 John 5:18).

- I am not the great "I Am" (Exodus 3:14, John 8:24, 28, 58), but by the grace of God, I am what I am (1 Colossians 15:10).

Anderson, N. T., & Park, D. (2007). Who am I? In *Stomping out the Darkness* (pp. 26-28). Bloomington MN: Bethany House Publishers.

Since I Am In Christ

- I am now acceptable to God (justified) and completely forgiven. I live at peace with Him (Romans 5:1).

- The sinful person I used to be died with Christ, and sin no longer rules my life (Romans 6:1-7).

- I am free from the punishment (condemnation) my sin deserves (Romans 8:1).

- I have been placed into Christ by God's doing (1 Corinthians 1:30).

- I have received God's Spirit into my life. I can recognize the blessings He has given me (1 Corinthians 2:12).

- I have been given the mind of Christ. He gives me wisdom to make right choices (1 Corinthians 2:16).

- I have been bought with a price; I am not my own; I belong to God (1 Corinthians 6:19-20).

- I am God's possession, chosen and secure (sealed) in Him; I have been given the Holy Spirit as a promise of my inheritance to come (2 Corinthians 1:21-22, Ephesians 1:13-14).

- Since I have died, I no longer live for myself, but for Christ (2 Corinthians 5:14-15).

- I have been made acceptable to God (righteous) (2 Corinthians 5:21).

- I have been blessed with every spiritual blessing (Ephesians 1:3).

- I was chosen in Christ to be holy before the world was created. I am without blame before Him (Ephesians 1:4).

- I was chosen by God (predestined) to be adopted as His child (Ephesians 1:5).

- I have been bought out of slavery to sin (redeemed) and forgiven (Ephesians 1:6,7).

- I have received His generous grace (Ephesians 1:7-8).

- I have been made spiritually alive just as Christ is alive (Ephesians 2:5).

- I have been raised up and seated with Christ in heaven (Ephesians 2:6).

- I have direct access to God through the Spirit (Ephesians 2:18).

- I may approach God with boldness, freedom, and confidence (Ephesians 3:12).

Anderson, N. T., & Park, D. (2007) Since I Am In Christ In *Stomping out the Darkness* (pp 34-36). Bloomington MN: Bethany House Publishers.

EPIC CHALLENGE

1. Have you ever felt like a prodigal child? In what ways have you run away from the Father?

2. Did it surprise you that God was waiting for you with open arms when you returned to Him?

3. The enemy has a strategy; what three things does he want to do to every believer in Christ? (See page 38)

4. The father gave the son a robe and put in on him; what is the spiritual significance of the robe?

5. You have been made righteous in Christ because of your union with Him. Identify the ways or degrees to which God makes us righteous:

    2 Corinthians 5:21

    1 Corinthians 6:11

    Hebrews 10:14

    Colossians 1:12

6. How do you feel after reviewing these verses?

7. What was the significance of the gift of the ring? What did it mean in ancient Israel?

8. What were the other two gifts from the father and what was their significance?

9. Read 1 Peter 2:5. This passage speaks about presenting gifts that are acceptable to God through Jesus Christ. What kind of gifts could you present to Christ today?

EPIC

Freedom

❖ Declaration against the enemy (out loud) ❖

By the power and the blood of the Lord Jesus Christ, I command, I don't suggest, I command any and all evil trying to influence me, my mind, or my body, to leave my presence. I am a child of the Most High God and my mind is my own, a quiet place for just me and God. I am free to hear the voice of God and pray as Jesus commanded us to pray.

❖ Prayer of Submission to God (out loud) ❖

Dear Heavenly Father, I know that You are here and present in my life and that You alone are all-powerful and mighty. I draw near to You and ask that You would draw near to me. I ask You to speak to me; I don't want to hear the words of man, I want to hear from You. Show me how to walk free today. In Jesus' name I pray, Amen.

What is real faith?

The Christian life is a walk of faith (2 Corinthians 5:7). It is necessary for salvation (Ephesians 2:8-9), for our spiritual growth (Colossians 2:7), and ministry (1 Timothy 1:12, 2 Timothy 2:2). Therefore, it is crucial that we as Christians understand what real faith is.

Faith means to put your complete trust or confidence in someone or something

Faith requires an object (Hebrews 11:6)

- We all live and operate by faith.
- The main difference between the Christian and the non-Christian is the object of their faith.
- Jesus is the only trustworthy object of our faith (John 14:6).

Everyone has been given a measure of faith (Romans 12:3)

- If you have trusted Christ as your Savior, you have already exhibited the greatest act of faith.
- If you think you lack faith, get into God's Word (Romans 10:17).
- A little faith goes a long way—a mustard seed can move a mountain (Matthew 17:20).

Faith looks at the facts

- Predictive prophecies that prove Jesus is the Messiah.
- Biblical evidence tests—you can trust your Bible!
- Jesus' life, death, and resurrection.

The importance of prophecy cannot be overstated. We have listed 40 prophecies in Appendix B, but there are many more. These prophecies are specific. For example, Micah 5:2 says the Messiah would be born in Bethlehem. Malachi 3:1 says He will be preceded by a forerunner.

In an article by Peter Stoner, the Chairman of the Department of Mathematics and Astronomy at Pasadena College, he looks at the mathematical possibility of one man fulfilling just eight of the over 300 prophecies about the coming Messiah. He found there was one chance in 10^{17} or 1,000,000,000,000,000,000 that one man could fulfill all eight. Stoner says if we add another 8, the probability is now 1 in 10^{45}. (Stoner, 1958)*. Since Jesus did fulfill them, prophecy shows that Jesus Christ is, in fact, the Messiah. However, we must still individually respond and receive Him as Savior by faith.

Check out Appendix B for more evidence, facts, and faith builders.

Faith in God grows as we get to know Him better (Romans 10:17)

- God will often put you in situations where you can learn to trust Him.
- Don't let thoughts against God develop!
- Don't let your faith get weak.
- Consider the traffic light illustration.

True faith results in actions

"Dear friends, do you think you'll get anywhere in this if you learn all the right words but never do anything? Does merely talking about faith indicate that a person really has it? For instance, you come upon an old friend dressed in rags and half-starved and say, 'Good morning, friend! Be clothed in Christ! Be filled with the Holy Spirit!' and walk off without providing so much as a coat or a cup of soup—where does that get you? Isn't it obvious that God-talk without God-acts is outrageous nonsense?

I can already hear one of you agreeing by saying, 'Sounds good. You take care of the faith department, I'll handle the works department.'

Not so fast. You can no more show me your works apart from your faith than I can show you my faith apart from my works. Faith and works, works and faith, fit together hand in glove" (James 2:14-18 The Message).

* Stoner, P and Newman, R. (Online edition 2005, November). *Science Speaks, Online Edition.* http://sciencespeaks.dstoner.net/index.html#c0

EPIC CHALLENGE

1. All people live by faith in something or someone. What is the object of your faith? Is it trustworthy? Why or why not?

2. Review the definition of "faith." Put the definition into your own words. Complete this sentence: "My faith in God grows when…"

3. Why is predictive prophecy so compelling when it comes to putting your trust in Jesus as the Messiah?

4. What prophecy about Jesus most surprises you personally? (See Appendix B)

5. How do we know that we can trust the Bible and know that it has not been tampered with? (See Appendix B)

6. Do you think the disciples would die for the cause of Christ if they knew he was actually dead and not resurrected? Explain. Who saw Jesus after His death on the cross?

7. Read Colossians 1:13. What did God deliver you from?

8. What is the most important truth you learned from this message?

"For though we walk in the flesh, we are not waging war according to the flesh. For the weapons of our warfare are not of the flesh but have divine power to destroy strongholds. We destroy arguments and every lofty opinion raised against the knowledge of God, and take every thought captive to obey Christ" (2 Corinthians 10:3-5).

Strongholds are destructive patterns of thought burned into our minds over time or from the intensity of traumatic experiences.

It would be nice if the strongholds in our minds were simply the result of all the garbage we fed into our brains when we were growing up. You know, "garbage in, garbage out."

If that were the case, all we would need would be some nice reprogramming through studying the Bible, good counseling, and more education. Certainly, those three things are a big part of breaking down strongholds, but there is more to the story. We have a spiritual enemy (the devil) who acts like a computer "virus," seeking to gum up the whole works.

Notice the following verses:

"Now when Jesus came into the district of Caesarea Philippi, he asked his disciples, 'Who do people say that the Son of Man is?' And they said, 'Some say John the Baptist, others say Elijah, and others Jeremiah or one of the prophets.' He said to them, 'But who do you say that I am?' Simon Peter replied, 'You are the Christ, the Son of the living God.' And Jesus answered him, 'Blessed are you, Simon Bar-Jonah! For flesh and blood has not revealed this to you, but my Father who is in heaven'" (Matthew 16:13-17).

"From that time Jesus began to show his disciples that he must go to Jerusalem and suffer many things from the elders and chief priests and scribes, and be killed, and on the third day be raised. And Peter took him aside and began to rebuke him, saying, 'Far be it from you, Lord! This shall never happen to you.' But he turned and said to Peter, 'Get behind me, Satan!'" (Matthew 16:21-23a).

Satan can put thoughts into our heads (Matthew 16)

How does Satan do this? Does he sit down face to face and say, "Now this is what I want you to do, David..."? Do we believe that King David would have numbered Israel if he thought it was Satan's idea (1 Chronicles 21:1)? Of course not! This idea was David's idea—*or at least he thought it was!*

The point is that Satan is capable of putting a thought in our minds in the first person singular. We actually believe the thought is our own! Hence, there is the necessity to take every thought captive to the obedience of Christ (2 Corinthians 10:5).

"During supper, when the devil had already put into the heart of Judas Iscariot, Simon's son, to betray him..." (John 13:2).

"But Peter said, 'Ananias, why has Satan filled your heart to lie to the Holy Spirit and keep back some of the price of the land?" (Acts 5:3).

"Then Satan stood up against Israel and incited David to number Israel" (1 Chronicles 21:1).

Understanding our thoughts

Paul admonishes us to take every thought (*noema*) captive to the obedience of Christ (2 Corinthians 10:5). Since nothing has meaning without context, how does Paul use the word *noema* in his writing?

- Unforgiveness – Satan's greatest access to the Church (2 Corinthians 2:10-11); "designs" or "schemes" (*noema*)

- Satan blinds the minds of the unbelieving (2 Corinthians 4:3-4); "minds" (*noema*)

- Keeping our focus on Christ (2 Corinthians 11:3); "thoughts" (*noema*)

Destroying Strongholds

- Be transformed by renewing your mind (Romans 12:2). Study the scriptures (2 Timothy 2:15). Let Christ's peace and word rule in your heart (Colossians 3:15-16).

- Prepare your mind for action (1 Peter 1:13). Keep your mind active and externally focused. Use "sanctified" imagination.

- Turn to God (Philippians 4:6-7).

- Choose to think the truth (Philippians 4:8).

It takes six weeks to develop a destructive habit!

It takes six weeks to develop a godly habit!

Taking Every Thought Captive

We must reject any thought that would turn us away from God and His Word, keep our focus on Christ (Hebrews 12:2), and our ears open to His voice (John 10:27-28).

The Choice Is Up To Us

- We act upon our choices.
- Repeated "low road" actions become bad habits.
- Our bad habits become strongholds.

> **Strongholds** are destructive patterns of thought burned into our minds over time or from the intensity of traumatic experiences. You can also develop godly strongholds! Ask the Lord to reveal to your mind any destructive habits or strongholds. Jesus is the bondage breaker, and He can and will tear down anything that stands between us and Him.

EPIC CHALLENGE

1. Give two biblical examples where Satan put his thoughts in a believer's mind.

2. Why would the devil want to plant a thought in your mind?

3. Why is it so important to take every thought captive?

4. Complete the following sentences:

   When the enemy puts thoughts in my mind I…

   To break down strongholds in my life I need to…

5. What is one good thing that I need to choose to do for the next six weeks so I can develop a godly habit?

6. The most important truth I learned from this message is...

Habits and Strongholds

When a habit and stronghold are formed, we lose our freedom.

Stimulation (from our environment)

- Brief (situations, places, pictures, etc.)
- Prevailing (family, friends, job, neighborhood, etc.)

1. Temptation (1 Corinthians 10:13)

Temptation begins with a seed thought that is essentially: "You can get your needs met through the world, the flesh, or the devil." The root of all temptation is to get the Christian to live independently of God. We maintain self-control by managing our thoughts at the threshold of perception.

People are not shaped by the environment, but by their perception of the environment. It is not life events that determine who we are, but how we interpret life events. The tendency is to believe that certain activating events are what determine how we act and feel.

"He made me so mad!" "What did you expect me to do in that situation?" "Any person with guts would have ripped him!" Statements like these say, "I have no control over my emotions or will."

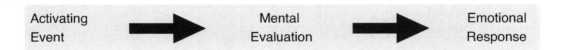

Activating Event → Mental Evaluation → Emotional Response

In reality, we have very little, if any, control over our emotions, but we do have control of our thought life, and our thoughts determine our feelings.

2. Consideration

Faith is God's way, and reason is man's way. It is not that faith is unreasonable because God is a rational God and does work through our reason. The problem is that man's ability to reason is limited. *"Trust in the LORD with all your heart, and do not lean on your own understanding"* (Proverbs 3:5). We consciously or subconsciously form two plans in our minds.

Plan A is God's way, which we accept by faith. The strength of plan A is dependent upon two things: (1) the person's conviction that God's way is right: and (2) the person's level of commitment to obeying God.

Plan B is humanistic reasoning, man's tendency to rationalize. The strength of plan B is determined by the amount of time one entertains thoughts that are contrary to the Word of God. Often, Plan B is a well-thought-out "escape route" should Plan A fail!

The greatest point of indecision is when the pull of both plans is about equal. An example of this type of thinking is a spouse who is no longer sure the present marriage will work. So the person begins to formulate Plan B just in case. The process always begins with a seed thought that results in behavioral changes. One spouse may, for instance, set aside money in a private bank account in order to survive if or when a divorce happens. Unfortunately, the possibility of a divorce is increased with each action taken based on Plan B. Proverbs 23:7 (NASB) says, *"For as he thinks within himself, so he is."*

3. Choice

Do I choose Plan A or Plan B? Do I choose the high road or the low road?

4. Act

Choices lead to actions.

5. Habit

Repeated actions form habits.

It takes six weeks to establish a habit.

6. Strongholds

Strongholds are mental patterns of thought burned into our minds over time or from the intensity of traumatic experiences. Strongholds are revealed in unChrist-like temperaments and behavior patterns often unrecognized by self, or if recognized, are seldom understood as a choice: *"So what if I'm an insensitive person—that's just the way I am!"*

Strongholds show up as ungodly traits and actions. For example, look at the following diagram:

Legitimate Need: Acceptance or Significance

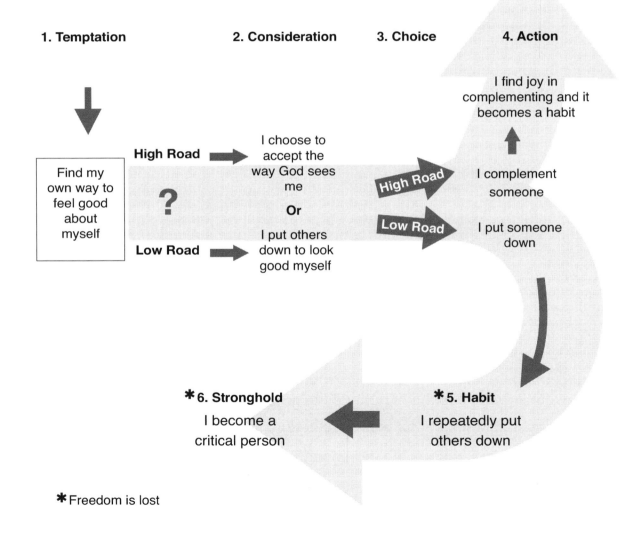

1. Temptation

2. Consideration

3. Choice

4. Action

Find my own way to feel good about myself

High Road — I choose to accept the way God sees me

?

Or

Low Road — I put others down to look good myself

High Road — I complement someone

Low Road — I put someone down

I find joy in complementing and it becomes a habit

*6. Stronghold
I become a critical person

*5. Habit
I repeatedly put others down

*Freedom is lost

We Must Break Down Strongholds

1. **Revelation** – Ask the Spirit to reveal the things that you need to repent of (John 8:32, John 16:13)

2. **Repent** – Confess the sin (2 Corinthians 7:10, 1 John 1:9)

3. **Receive** – Receive God's promised forgiveness (Acts 3:19-20, 1 John 1:9)

4. **Renounce** – Renounce the lie (Proverbs 28:13, 2 Corinthians 4:2)

5. **Resist** – Resist the enemy (James 4:7)

6. **Renew** your mind with God's Word (Romans 12:2)
   - God's Word is powerful and true (Hebrews 4:12, Jeremiah 23:29, John 8:32, Psalm 119:160.
   - Study God's Word (2 Timothy 2:15)
   - Let the Word of Christ richly dwell within you (Colossians 3:15-16)

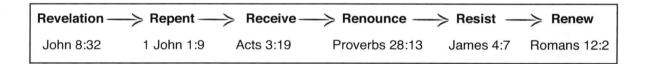

Revelation	Repent	Receive	Renounce	Resist	Renew
John 8:32	1 John 1:9	Acts 3:19	Proverbs 28:13	James 4:7	Romans 12:2

Twenty Cans of Success

1. Why should I say, "I can't" when the Bible says, *"I can do all things through Him (Christ) who strengthens me"* (Philippians 4:13)?

2. Why should I worry about my needs when *"...God shall supply all (my) needs according to His riches in glory in Christ Jesus"* (Philippians 4:19)?

3. Why should I fear when the Bible says that *"...God did not give (me) a spirit of timidity, but a spirit of power, of love and of self-discipline"* (2 Timothy 1:7)?

4. Why should I doubt or lack faith to live for Christ knowing that *"...God has allotted to each a measure of faith"* (Romans 12:3)?

5. Why should I be weak when the Bible says, *"The Lord is the strength of my life"* (Psalm 27:1, NKJ) and *"... people who know their God will display strength..."* (Daniel 11:32)?

6. Why should I allow Satan to have supremacy over my life, for *"greater is He who is in you than he who is in the world"* (1 John 4:4)?

7. Why should I accept defeat when the Bible says, *"...thanks be to God, who always leads us in His triumph in Christ..."* (2 Corinthians 2:14)?

8. Why should I lack wisdom when *"...you are in Christ Jesus, who became to us wisdom from God,"* (1 Corinthians 1:30) and *"If any of you lacks wisdom, let him ask God, who gives to all generously and without reproach"* (James 1:5)?

9. Why should I be depressed when I can recall to my mind and therefore have hope: *"the Lord's loving-kindnesses...never cease, for His compassions never fail. They are new every morning; great is Thy faithfulness"* (Lamentations 3:21-23)?

10. Why should I worry and fret when I am told to *"cast all your anxiety upon Him, because He cares for you"* (1 Peter 5:7 NIV)?

11. Why should I ever be in bondage, for *"...where the Spirit of the Lord is, there is freedom"* (2 Corinthians 3:17) and *"it was for freedom that Christ set us free"* (Galatians 5:1)?

12. Why should I feel condemned when the Bible says, *"Therefore there is now no condemnation for those who are in Christ Jesus"* (Romans 8:1)?

13. Why should I ever feel alone when Jesus said *"...I am with you always, even to the end of the age"* (Matthew 28:20) and *"I will never desert you, nor will I ever forsake you"* (Hebrews 13:5)?

14. Why should I feel like I'm cursed or the victim of bad luck when the Bible says that *"Christ redeemed us from the curse of Law, having become a curse for us...in order that in Christ Jesus... we might receive the promise of the Spirit through faith"* (Galatians 3:13-14)?

15. Why should I be discontented when I, like Paul, can *"...learn to be content in whatever the circumstances"* (Philippians 4:11 NIV)?

16. Why should I feel worthless when *"(God) made Him who knew no sin to be sin on our behalf, so that we might become the righteousness of God in Him"* (2 Corinthians 5:21)?

17. Why should I feel helpless around others when I know that *"... if God is for us, who is against us"* (Romans 8:31)?

18. Why should I be confused when *"now we have received, not the spirit of the world, but the Spirit who is from God, that we might know the things freely given to us by God"* (1 Corinthians 2:12)? And *"...God is not a God of confusion but of peace"* (1 Corinthians 14:33)?

19. Why should I feel like a failure when *"...in all these things we overwhelmingly conquer through Him who loved us"* (Romans 8:37)?

20. Why should I let the pressures of life bother me when Jesus said, *"...In the world you have tribulation, but take courage; I have overcome the world"* (John 16:33)?

Anderson, N. T., & Park, D. (2007). Twenty Cans of Success In *Stomping out the Darkness* (pp. 71-72). Bloomington MN: Bethany House Publishers.

EPIC CHALLENGE

1. What is real Biblical repentance?

2. Read 2 Corinthians 7:10 and 1 John 1:9. What role does confession play in real repentance?

3. Why is repentance not enough to break a stronghold?

4. Read Proverbs 28:13. What is the difference between confession and renunciation?

5. How do you renew your mind? What role does the Word of God play?

6. Read Colossians 3:15-16. What do these verses tell us to do with God's Word?

7. How do we resist the enemy? Read James 4:7.

8. What is the greatest stronghold in your life?

9. What positive stronghold would you like to develop in your life?

10. Read through the Twenty Cans of Success for the next 40 days.

Forgiveness is required by God (Matthew 6:9-15)

Forgiveness is crucial for our freedom

"Then Peter came up and said to him, 'Lord, how often will my brother sin against me, and I forgive him? As many as seven times?' Jesus said to him, 'I do not say to you seven times, but seventy-seven times.

Therefore the kingdom of heaven may be compared to a king who wished to settle accounts with his servants. When he began to settle, one was brought to him who owed him ten thousand talents. And since he could not pay, his master ordered him to be sold, with his wife and children and all that he had, and payment to be made. So the servant fell on his knees, imploring him, 'Have patience with me, and I will pay you everything.' And out of pity for him, the master of that servant released him and forgave him the debt.

But when that same servant went out, he found one of his fellow servants who owed him a hundred denarii, and seizing him, he began to choke him, saying, 'Pay what you owe.' So his fellow servant fell down and pleaded with him, 'Have patience with me, and I will pay you.' He refused and went and put him in prison until he should pay the debt. When his fellow servants saw what had taken place, they were greatly distressed, and they went and reported to their master all that had taken place.

Then his master summoned him and said to him, 'You wicked servant! I forgave you all that debt because you pleaded with me. And should not you have had mercy on your fellow servant, as I had mercy on you?' And in anger his master delivered him to the jailers, until he should pay all his debt. So also my heavenly Father will do to every one of you, if you do not forgive your brother from your heart'" (Matthew 18:21-35).

- We need to know the extent of our debt to God
- Realize repaying God is impossible
- Understand the need for God's mercy
- We forgive to avoid God's discipline

Forgiveness is to be extended to others (Ephesians 4:31-32)
We forgive because we are forgiven. Forgiving others is between us and God.

Why should we forgive?

- TO STOP THE PAIN! (Jonah)
- So that Satan does not take advantage of us (2 Corinthians 2:10-11)

Forgiveness is NOT:

- Forgetting

- Excusing sin

Forgiveness is:

- Choosing not to take revenge

- Choosing not to hold another's sin against them

- Looking for justice in the cross of Christ

- An act of love (1 Corinthians 13:5)

Story of Forgiveness

One of the most inspiring stories of forgiveness is that of the late Corrie ten Boom. Corrie, a Christian Dutch woman, was imprisoned, beaten, and humiliated in a Nazi concentration camp during World War II. After the war, she returned to Germany to preach the good news of God's forgiveness.

At the close of a service in 1947, Corrie's message of forgiveness was put to a severe test. As people filed out of the church, one man came forward to talk to her. She recognized him immediately as one of the guards from the prison. She thought about his whip and his uniform with the skull and crossbones on the cap. She remembered the shame of walking naked past him with thousands of women prisoners. She remembered her sister's slow, terrible death there. Her blood seemed to freeze.

Corrie tried to avoid talking to him, hoping he wouldn't remember her. But he identified himself as a guard at the camp where she had been. He said, "Since that time I have become a Christian, I know that God has forgiven me for the cruel things I did there." Then he stuck out his hand. "Will you forgive me?"

She stood there with coldness clutching her heart. She didn't want to forgive him. She didn't feel like forgiving him. But she knew forgiveness is an act of the will, not an emotion. "Jesus, help me!" she prayed silently. "I can lift my hand. I can do that much. You supply the feeling."

Almost mechanically she reached out to grasp his hand. As they joined hands, a healing warmth seemed to flood her whole being, bringing tears to her eyes, "I forgive you, brother!" she cried. "With my whole heart!"

The former guard and the former prisoner grasped each other's hands for a long moment. Forgiveness had healed the hurts of the past.

Adapted from a tract by Good News Publisher, Westchester, IL. (This story also appears in the book *Stomping Out The Darkness* by Neil Anderson and Dave Park).

Steps to Forgiveness

1. Pray and ask God to reveal to you all the people you need to forgive.

2. Make a list of all those names, including perhaps Mom, Dad, yourself, etc.

3. Admit the hurt or hatred you may have felt.

4. Decide you will bear with the consequences of their sin(s) and not hold it against them in the future.

5. Accept Christ's death as full payment for their sin (Romans 5:17-18).

6. Let God deal with their sin as He sees fit (Romans 12:19).

7. Make the choice to forgive.

EPIC CHALLENGE

1. Why is it so important to forgive?

2. Review the definition of "forgiveness." Put the definition in your own words.

3. Do you struggle with forgiving those who hurt you? Why do you think it is so hard sometimes?

4. What did you think of the story of Corrie ten Boom?

5. God says that it is wrong to take revenge. Why does He forbid us to do so?

6. The most important truth I learned from this message is…

"And you shall remember the whole way that the LORD your God has led you these forty years in the wilderness, that he might humble you, testing you to know what was in your heart, whether you would keep his commandments or not" (Deuteronomy 8:2).

God's Voice in the Desert

- God speaks.

- God puts you in an environment where you can best hear Him.

- Let the desert bring brokenness and surrender.

- Beyond salvation, God wants you to experience freedom, so He wants to reveal what is in your heart.

How do you know when you are in a desert?

- It's suddenly uncomfortable.

- Everything has changed – The old ways don't work.

- Nothing satisfies your thirst.

Why did they wander?

The journey should have taken 6 weeks, instead it took 40 years.

"Now when all the people saw the thunder and the flashes of lightning and the sound of the trumpet and the mountain smoking, the people were afraid and trembled, and they stood far off and said to Moses, "You speak to us, and we will listen; but do not let God speak to us, lest we die." Moses said to the people, "Do not fear, for God has come to test you, that the fear of him may be before you, that you may not sin" (Exodus 20:18-20).

God did not want a distant relationship with us, but rather, He desires a personal, intimate relation with us. God allows us to wander, so we can learn to hear His voice.

Wandering: The Hebrew word (Ta`ah).

Definition: to err, wander, go astray, stagger

(Qal) to err
- to wander about
  (*physically*)
- of intoxication
- of sin (*ethically*)
- wandering (*of the mind*)

(Niphal)
- to be made to wander about,
  be made to stagger
  (*drunkard*)
- to be led astray (*ethically*)

(Hiphal)
- to cause to wander about
  (*physically*)
- to cause to wander (*of
  intoxication*)
- to cause to err, mislead
  (*mentally and morally*)

Background

Deuteronomy 6:4-5 introduces to the children of Israel how God wanted them to pray or more importantly, hear from Him.

This prayer is called the Shema, which means to "hear." It is the Hebrew word that begins the most significant prayer in Judaism. This prayer begins with the command to "Hear to Obey."

Hear, O Israel: The LORD our God, the LORD is one. You shall love the LORD your God with all your heart and with all your soul and with all your might. And these words that I command you today shall be on your heart. You shall teach them diligently to your children, and shall talk of them when you sit in your house, and when you walk by the way, and when you lie down, and when you rise. You shall bind them as a sign on your hand, and they shall be as frontlets between your eyes. You shall write them on the doorposts of your house and on your gates.

- The Children of Israel were delivered from slavery out of Egypt (saved), but they were still not personally hearing the voice of God. They were not experiencing intimacy with God.

- God may send us to the wilderness (desert) to humble us and create brokenness and surrender in our hearts.

- The children of Israel wandered for 40 years, but they refused to let God show them what was in their hearts. That generation died out; only Joshua and Caleb entered the promised land. (Numbers 32:13)

- We must discover what is in our hearts, both sin and righteous pursuits.

- We cannot discover what is in our hearts by self-revelation or personal examination; we must have an encounter with God. Only by divine relation or hearing from His voice can we truly discover what is in our hearts and walk in freedom.

Some important Hebrew wordplay:

- The Hebrew word for wilderness or deserts is מדבר. The Hebrew term for God speaking is מדבר.

- Can you spot the difference between the two words? There isn't any – it's from the same word root.

- The word for *desert* is pronounced "***midbar***" in Hebrew and the Hebrew for *speaking* is pronounced "***medaber***."

- Simply put, God sends us to the <u>desert</u> (Midbar) so we can hear <u>His voice</u> (Midbar).

- Midbar or wilderness occurs nearly 300 times in the Bible.

- Midbar means mouth or voice, as an organ of speech.

> *"Therefore, I am now going to allure her; I will lead her into the wilderness and speak tenderly to her."* (Hosea 2:14)

God does not want to take you to the desert to give you a spiritual spanking or lecture; He wants to allure you to a place and position where you can hear His voice. When God takes you to the desert, He then speaks tenderly and shows you what is in your heart (your belief system). Deuteronomy 8:2 helps us deal with every hard "Why" question we have had in our lives.

- Why did my parents get a divorce?

- Why did I lose my child?

- Why did my loved one die?

- Why does God seem so distant?

While God isn't always responsible for the bad things in our lives, He always uses them.

God desires to show us what is in our hearts! Both good and bad! Will you let Him speak, or will you continue to wander? The choice is yours and yours alone. God will not make you. He may place you in the desert (midbar) the perfect place for you to hear Him, but He will not make you (midbar) hear Him and discover what's in your heart if you don't want to.

- Do you want to experience just escaping your bondage (Egypt), or do you wish to encounter true intimacy with God?

- God not only wants you to see what is in your heart; He also wants to show you what is in His heart.

- God wants to show you His promises.

Next Step:

As you go through the Lord's Prayer Journey in the next section of this workbook, let God speak to you and show you what is in your heart. This allows you to walk out your new identity as a child of God and experience the freedom that is found in Christ.

- Invite God to speak to you – His word and Spirit will reveal what's in your heart.

- Listen to Obey – Get ready to follow His ways, even if they are new ways.

- Don't just listen once, but like the Shema Prayer, make it a daily practice.

EPIC CHALLENGE

1. Describe a time when you were in the 'desert' or you felt like you were wandering.

2. Did you hear God speak to you in that desert? What did He say?

3. If you didn't hear God, do you think it was it because He wasn't speaking or you weren't listening?

4. What did we learn from Hosea 2:14 about how God speaks to us?

5. Take time and ask God to speak now about a current or past desert experience. He loves to talk with his children.

    What is God revealing to you about the hidden things in your heart?

    What has God showing you about His heart?

Dedication

This book, or rather tool, is dedicated to all those who long to be closer to Jesus! This book is also dedicated to Neil T. Anderson whose thumbprint you will see all over this Journey. Neil, most of what I share is simply a reiteration of what I heard you teach. Thank you for being such a great friend. Lastly, this work is dedicated to David and Allison Park, Mark and Ashley Baker, and Joey and Dani Bruno. You are the best children a father and mother could ever hope to have. It has been such a joy to watch you follow the Lord and serve Him. Thank you for giving us so many grand-babies!

Jesus told the story of a man who found a great hidden treasure in a field and happily sold everything he owned to be able to purchase the plot of land (Matthew 13:44). He was zealous about obtaining it, and nothing was going to stop him from getting it. This parable focuses on the incredible discovery of God and His kingdom and how, like the man in Jesus' story, we should be passionate about God and His kingdom. You could say that God desires that we have one passion, God, and God alone. That is what this Journey is all about! We seek a treasure, not of mere gold and silver held in earthen vessels, but Jesus the Christ, God Himself!

If you have put your faith and trust in Jesus Christ as your personal Savior, you are His beloved child and have eternal life (1 John 5:13). Being a child of God means we have special privileges. You can boldly approach the throne of God and receive mercy and find grace to help us in times of trouble (Hebrew 4:16). Jesus paid the full price for your sin on the cross, and He has set you free from sin and Satan's power by overcoming both sin and death through His sacrifice on the cross and resurrection. If you are not experiencing daily victory in your Christian walk, it may be because you have not realized fully what it means to be a child of God and how to overcome the world, the flesh, and the devil.

1 Timothy 4:7 says to *"train yourself for godliness."* Godliness is God's standard for His child. He has made you holy, like Jesus, and desires that you live like Him. You have been made holy, that was God's gift to you, but He doesn't want anything to keep you from displaying your holiness. It is your responsibility to do whatever is necessary to follow after or pursue righteousness, godliness, faith, and love (1 Timothy 6:11).

You will be following Christ's model for prayer, as found in Matthew 6:9-13, commonly known as the Lord's Prayer. You will use the truth and biblical principles He outlined in this prayer as a guide to help you experience the full victory that Jesus promised His children. Do not expect someone else to pray these prayers for you, or renounce your personal lies and deceptions. Only you can do this. However, we strongly recommend that a mature Christian is with you as you go through this Prayer Journey (a trusted friend, a pastor, a counselor, etc.).

This is a Holy Spirit experience. Great peace and personal victory will result from what you choose to believe, confess, declare, forgive, and renounce. No one can choose the truth for you, but Jesus told us that the Spirit would lead us into all truth. Freedom can only be gained as YOU choose truth. Truth opens a passageway to abiding in Christ, a place where you can know God and experience His great love for you. The freedom to worship God in fullness and obey His commands is brought to life. This means you will have the power to say, "no" to the world, the flesh, and the devil. The

Christian life is a life of growth and abiding in Christ. It is not a life of sinless perfection. God alone can meet your deepest personal and emotional needs for identity, approval, protection, provision, belonging, meaning, and importance. All of these are themes in the Lord's Prayer.

Not a Formula

This Prayer Journey and the Lord's Prayer are not a formula or a canned counseling method. This Prayer Journey does not set you free. Christ sets you free. Your response to Him - turning from sin and abiding in Christ - works this freedom in you. While the Journey and the prayers are not to be used as *'empty phrases'* (Matthew 6:7), they are a powerful pathway into God's presence and a way to experience His abiding love. They will help you examine your life to see if any strongholds or lies have invaded your belief system. King David said in Psalm 139:23-24, *"Search me, O God, and know my heart...see if there be any grievous way in me..."* This Prayer Journey provides you with a unique opportunity to have an incredible encounter with God. He is our Wonderful Counselor and friend.

Safe In Christ

You are safe and secure in Christ. God has sealed us with His Spirit. 1 John 5:13-15 says, *"I write these things to you who believe in the name of the Son of God, that you may know that you have eternal life. And this is the confidence we have toward him, that if we ask anything according to his will, he hears us. And if we know that he hears us in whatever we ask, we know that we have the requests that we have asked of him."* 1 John 4:4 states that, *"...greater is he who is in you than he who is in the world."* We are safe and secure in Christ's loving arms. These are not true just because we believe them—we believe them because they are true. They are God's promises to you! As you go through the Journey remember these truths.

If you are struggling with a stronghold, God has blessed us with this truth in 1 John 1:9; *"If we confess our sins, he is faithful and just to forgive us our sins and to cleanse us from all unrighteousness."* We are also told in Ephesians 4:27, *"...and give no opportunity to the devil."* Remember, we have everything we need in Christ. Truth tells us that we are safe in Christ. Truth also says, *"Then You will know the truth, and the truth will set you free."* (John 8:32).

The Battle for the Mind

As you go through this Prayer Journey, you may experience any number of destructive thoughts in your mind to try to get you to stop praying. Don't listen to any of them. They are simply lies from the enemy designed to get you to give up and go back to your old way of living. They can only stop you if you accept them as true. But they are not true, so reject them and move on. If another Christian is working with you, as we recommend, share with that person any thoughts which tempt you to give up. As soon as you reveal the lie, the power of Satan is broken.

Remember that Satan will only be defeated if you confront him aloud. He doesn't have to obey your thoughts. Only God knows perfectly what is going on in your mind. As you process each part of the Lord's Prayer and this Journey, it is important that you submit to God in your heart and then resist the devil by reading aloud each prayer and statement (James 4:7).

So find a private place where you can pray out loud.

While the Prayer Journey can play a big part in your process of becoming more like Christ and following Him, there is no such thing as a one time experience or event that will instantly transform you into His image. Discipleship is a lifelong process. It takes time to destroy old habits and create new ones. The more time you spend in God's word, praying, and abiding in Christ, the more your mind will be transformed.

Paul wrote, *"Do not be conformed to this world, but be transformed by the renewal of your mind"* (Romans 12:2). This Prayer Journey will help you break away from the world's patterns and establish new Christ-like habits.

No matter where you are in your walk with the Lord, you have nothing to lose and possibly everything to gain by praying through this Prayer Journey. If your troubles come from a cause other than those covered by the Lord's Prayer and the Biblical principles outlined in the Prayer Journey, you may need to get further help. The real focus here is your relationship with God and abiding in Christ.

God Will Guide You

The Lord's Prayer Journey contains ten petitions. Each of these petitions contains many roots like a tall, powerful tree. Take the time to examine each root issue under each petition. Psalm 1:1-3 says, "Blessed *is the man who walks not in the counsel of the wicked, nor stands in the way of sinners, nor sits in the seat of scoffers; but his delight is in the law of the Lord, and on his law he meditates day and night. He is like a tree planted by streams of water that yields its fruit in its season, and its leaf does not wither. In all that he does, he prospers."*

Today, it is as if you are sitting at the feet of Jesus and praying as He instructed His disciples to pray. You are about to spend a deep and extensive time in meditation and prayer. Each petition and its various roots are explained, so you will have no problem knowing what to do or pray. If one of the root issues does not apply to you, simply pass over that section. Be careful not to be deceived and pass over an issue you might truly need to pray through for spiritual breakthrough. No matter what you have done or what has been done to you, you can go through this Prayer Journey. If you experience any kind of resistance, stop and use your authority in Christ. Tell the enemy to leave your presence. Remember that God is always with you. He promised to never leave you (Matthew 28:20). Don't believe the lie that you are too spiritually weak to go through this Prayer Journey, because the Bible says, "I can *do all things through him who strengthens me"* (Philippians 4:13). If you experience random thoughts in your mind, just ignore them. A thought can have no power over you unless you believe it. Don't believe it! Don't go off on mental rabbit trails. Stay focused on what God's word is asking you to believe and pray.

As you go through the Prayer Journey please pray out loud every section in the shaded boxes. It is not necessary to read aloud the words in parentheses. They are there to explain a meaning or give the Biblical reference. It is our prayer that God will reveal Himself to you in a powerful way, that you will experience His great love for you, that you will walk away cleansed and forgiven, and that you will experience real freedom in your Christian life.

We encourage you to share what you have experienced with others so that they might experience the peace you have found.

Begin the EPIC Journey with this Declaration and Prayer!

❖ Declaration against the enemy (out loud) ❖

By the power and the blood of the Lord Jesus Christ, I command, I don't suggest, I command any and all evil in or around this place, trying to influence me, my mind, or my body, to leave my presence. You cannot touch or harm me. I am a child of the Most High God (John1:12) and my mind is my own; a quiet place for just me and God. I am free to hear the voice of God and pray as Jesus commanded us to pray.

❖ Prayer of Submission to God (out loud) ❖

Dear Heavenly Father, I know that You are here with me now. I believe that You alone are all-knowing, all-powerful and ever-present. I declare that I need You and without You I can do nothing. The Bible is Your word; it is God-breathed and tells me what is really true. I refuse to believe the lies of Satan. I stand in the truth that all authority in heaven and on earth has been given the risen Christ. I ask You to protect my thoughts and mind, to fill me with Your Holy Spirit, and to lead me into all truth. So with confidence I pray:

Our Father in heaven, Hallowed be Your name. Your kingdom come. Your will be done On earth as it is in heaven. Give us this day our daily bread. And forgive us our debts, as we forgive our debtors. And do not lead us into temptation, But deliver us from the evil one. For Yours is the kingdom and the power and the glory forever, Amen (Matthew 6:9-13 NKJV).

"Our Father in heaven"

The first petition or request of God is that you might know Him personally as "Abba Father." "Abba" is the Aramaic word for daddy, that close and intimate childlike reference to one's father. God is, first of all, Father. His role as Father is one of the most significant aspects of His nature. Understanding the Father nature of God and His character is essential if you are to love God and be assured of His love for you. God expressed Himself as the Father who gave His only begotten Son to die for you (John 3:16). Failure to remove any misconception about the Father will greatly hinder your worship of Him, trusting Him, praying to Him and yielding to Him. God wants you to receive Him as your Father, to be able to spend time with Him and His word. Jesus came to show us the Father and make it possible for us to have a relationship with Him. When Jesus modeled for His disciples how to pray, He began, "Our Father." In the last hours of Jesus' life as He prayed the longest prayer recorded in the Bible, Jesus addressed God as "Father" six times (John 17).

While Jesus was in the Garden of Gethsemane, He prayed that the terrible hour of His separation from the Father might be taken away. Jesus said, *"Remove this cup from me. Yet not what I will, but what you will"* (Mark 14:36). Nothing was more important or more valuable to Jesus than being with the Father and being in His presence. Not being able to fellowship or abide in the Father was unthinkable to Jesus. When Jesus fell to the ground and prayed that this terrible hour of separation from the Father might pass from Him, He called upon the Father and said, "Abba Father" (Mark 14:35-36).

Sometimes we are impeded in our spiritual growth because we believe lies about God, or we have allowed thoughts against God to control our view or perception of who God is and how He relates to us. He is your "Abba Father," your "Daddy." You are no longer to fear His punishment or be distant from Him.

"For you did not receive the spirit of slavery to fall back into fear, but you have received the Spirit of adoption as sons, by whom we cry, "Abba! Father!" The Spirit himself bears witness with our spirit that we are children of God" (Romans 8:15-16).

"But when the fullness of time had come, God sent forth his Son, born of woman, born under the law, to redeem those who were under the law, so that we might receive adoption as sons. And because you are sons, God has sent the Spirit of his Son into our hearts, crying, 'Abba! Father!' So you are no longer a slave, but a son, and if a son, then an heir through God" (Galatians 4:4-7).

The following prayers are designed to help you experience a full relationship with your "Abba" Father, so you are free to abide and fellowship with Him. Begin this petition by praying aloud the following prayer:

❖ Our Father in Heaven ❖

I confess that I have not always felt close to You. I have not always experienced an intimate personal relationship with You. I realize now that I have kept You at a distance even though Your arms were always wide open to me (Romans 5:8). I desire to have a close "Abba" Father relationship with You. I know that I am Your dearly loved child (Romans 8:15-16), regardless of what my feelings might tell me. I choose to believe You and Your word. You have said, *"Behold, I stand at the door and knock; if anyone hears my voice and opens the door, I will come in to him and will eat with him, and he with me"* (Revelation 3:20). Father, today I open the door of my heart to You. I ask You now to reveal to my mind any lies I have believed about You or any thoughts I have held against You. In Jesus' name I pray, Amen.

Many people struggle with the concept of God as a loving, heavenly Father because their relationship with their earthly father is or was damaged. If your earthly father abused or abandoned you, was emotionally distant or aloof, or just hard to relate to, you may have great difficulty trusting your Heavenly Father. God created the family to reflect the heavenly reality of our relationship with Him. Unfortunately, every family and father is imperfect and fails in some way to live out God's purpose. However, God is perfect, and we are not to carry our view of our earthly father onto our loving Heavenly Father. Take care to destroy any negative thoughts or feelings toward God. List any events/circumstances in your life that have played a part in shaping your view or perception of God. For example, "If you're a good God, why did my parents get a divorce?" or "God, if you love me, why didn't you rescue me from that (tragic event)?"

The following questions are designed to help you become aware of any thoughts against God that you might be holding on to:

Have you ever felt angry or mad at God? Why? What happened to make you feel that way?

Do you love Jesus and the Holy Spirit but feel indifferent to God the Father?

Have you ever felt abandoned by God or that He has failed you?

Sometimes we tend to view our Heavenly Father according to our perceptions of our earthly father. How has your earthly father affected your current view of God the Father?

Can you recall to your mind a time when God has blessed you, or do you feel neglected or even cursed?

Do you feel other Christians have a more favorable relationship with God than you?

Do you ever feel like God the Father is a condemning and unforgiving judge?

Do you feel a sense of guilt and condemnation when you think of God the Father?

Have you ever cursed God out of anger or turned your back on Him?

Once you have prayerfully thought through these questions, confess and renounce each item or thought that has given you a false view of God. 2 Corinthians 10:5 says, "*We destroy arguments and every lofty opinion raised against the knowledge of God, and take every thought captive to obey Christ.*" Pray the following prayer aloud to help you destroy each argument against God and take it captive.

❖ Dear Heavenly Father ❖

I confess that I have believed lies from the enemy about You and had bad thoughts against You, my loving Heavenly Father. I know that I can never be close to You if I hold onto destructive thoughts against You. So I choose now to demolish every argument and every pretension that sets itself up against the knowledge of You and take every thought captive in obedience to Christ. Right now I specifically renounce the lie I have believed that You are _____. Thank You that in Christ I am forgiven. In Jesus' name I pray, Amen.

Prayerfully consider the following lists and mark all those that God reveals have been lies or thoughts you have had against God. After going through each checklist, take time to pray, confess your thoughts, expose the lies you have believed, and announce the truth about your Father.

My relationship with my "Abba" Father

I have not known God as:

_____ the perfect Father I have always desired.

_____ "Abba" daddy or Papa-God or received His loving parental affection.

_____ an absolutely faithful Father I could trust.

_____ a generous, giving daddy.

_____ an accepting Father and rested securely in Him.

_____ an attentive daddy who gives me special attention.

_____ Other ways I have seen God incorrectly_____.

> Father, I confess that I have not known or trusted You as _____ and I renounce this awful lie. I announce that I see You as my loving and caring Father. In Jesus' name I pray, Amen.

Yielding to Father God

I have not yielded to God's:

_____ gentle parental authority as Father God.

_____ guidance and Fatherhood.

_____ strength and accepted that I am secure in My Father's hand.

_____ right to be my Father through the blood of Jesus Christ.

_____ Other_____.

> Father, I confess that I have not yielded to You by failing to see Your_____. I yield to You and Your great love now and receive all You are as God my Father. In Jesus' name I pray, Amen.

Spiritual check list of lies about your Father God

I have believed the lie that:

_____ God was far-away, remote, and unreachable.

_____ I was set far away from, isolated, and secluded from God.

_____ God is indifferent to my problems and needs.

_____ God is insensitive and indifferent toward me.

_____ God is cold and callous toward me and my needs.

_____ God is strict and demanding when it comes to my behavior.

_____ God doesn't view me as special or important to Him.

_____ God gives favor to other believers more than me.

_____ God is absent and too busy for me.

_____ No matter what I do, God is dissatisfied with me.

_____ God is angry with me and wants to judge me.

_____ God is mean, vindictive, violent, and at times unfair.

_____ God is trying to take all the joy and peace out of my life.

_____ God is controlling and manipulative.

_____ God is critical and intolerant toward me and my sin.

_____ God is demanding and always trying to find my faults.

_____ Other_____

Father, I renounce the lie that You are _____ and I announce that You love and care for me and always do what is best for me. In Jesus' name I pray, Amen.

"'For I know the plans I have for you,' declares the LORD, 'plans for welfare and not for evil, to give you a future and a hope'" (Jeremiah 29:11).

"The LORD your God is in your midst, a mighty one who will save; he will rejoice over you with gladness; he will quiet you by his love; he will exult over you with loud singing" (Zephaniah 3:17).

"See what kind of love the Father has given to us, that we should be called children of God; and so we are..." (1 John 3:1).

Declaration of the Father's Heart

Your heavenly Father knew you before you were born (Psalm 139:13-16) and has always loved you. He has awesome plans for you (Jeremiah 29:11). Prepare now to proclaim aloud the truth about your awesome Father. If you have any trouble with a statement or cannot say it wholeheartedly, stop and look up the listed reference.

I believe that my Heavenly Father:

- loves me with an everlasting love (Jeremiah 31:3)
- loved and chose me before the foundation of the world (Ephesians 1:4-6)
- totally and unconditionally accepts me and loves me just as I am (Ephesians 1:4-6)
- will not let anything separate me from His love (Romans 8:35-39)
- will never abandon me, leave me or forsake me (Hebrews 13:5)

I believe that my Heavenly Father:

- is my "Abba" Father, daddy, Papa-God and that I am His beloved child (Galatians 4:4-7)
- has given me a special inheritance and made me a fellow heir with His Son Jesus (Romans 8:16-17)
- only wants what is best for me and the highest good (2 Thessalonians 1:11)
- only disciplines me with love and justice (Hebrews 12:6-11)
- gathers me in His loving arms and carries me all my life (Isaiah 40:11)

I believe that my Heavenly Father:

- is entirely stable and unchanging (Hebrews 13:8)
- is absolutely trustworthy and responsible (Isaiah 12:2)
- will never lie to me (Hebrews 6:18) and keeps all of His promises (2 Peter 1:4)
- will never fail me or fall short of meeting my needs (Psalm 89:33-34)
- knows all my needs (Matthew 6:8) and will meet them according to His riches in Christ (Philippians 4:19)

I believe that my Heavenly Father:

- ❖ is my Redeemer and Savior, who bought me back from my past life of sin (Isaiah 63:16)

- ❖ does not recall my sins and iniquities or choose to hold them against me (Hebrews 8:12)

- ❖ gives me peace and doesn't want me to be anxious or worry about anything (Philippians 4:7)

- ❖ bears all my burdens because He cares for me (1 Peter 5:7)

- ❖ will vindicate me (Psalm 7:8) and execute vengeance for me so I can rest in peace (Hebrews 10:30)

- ❖ gives me rest (Matthew 11:28-30) and revives me when I am tired and weary (Psalm 119:107)

I believe that my Heavenly Father:

- ❖ has blessed me with every spiritual blessing in the heavenly realms (Ephesians 1:3)

- ❖ lavishes me with His grace (Ephesians 1:7-8)

- ❖ exults over me with great joy and singing (Zephaniah 3:17)

- ❖ honors and cherishes me (Isaiah 43:3) and was pleased to make me His own (1 Samuel 12:22)

- ❖ keeps me from evil (1 Peter 2:25)

- ❖ takes great pleasure in me (Psalm 149:4)

"Hallowed be Your name"

The word "hallowed" means "holy." While there are hundreds of names for God in the Bible, Jesus is reminding us that whatever title or name we select from God's word, we must identify God with one dominant characteristic of His being — His holiness. God is, has been, and always will be holy (James 1:17). To be holy is to be sacred and set apart (sanctified). 1 Chronicles 16:10 says, *"Glory in his holy name: let the hearts of those who seek the LORD rejoice!"* Psalm 145:21 says, *"My mouth will speak in praise of the LORD, and let all flesh bless his holy Name forever and ever."* 1 John 1:5 states, *"This is the message we have heard from him and proclaim to you, that God is light, and in him there is no darkness at all."* Jesus is asking you to declare the holiness of God the Father as an act of worship.

> ### ❖ Dear Heavenly Father ❖
>
> I have not always worshiped You as I should and glorified Your holy name. I want my mouth to speak Your praises, so I ask You now to reveal to my mind which of Your wonderful names You would have me pray back to You today. In Jesus' name I pray, Amen.

____ Adonai	Master or Lord (Malachi 1:6)
____ Elohim	Eternal God (Genesis 2:3)
____ El Bethel	God is my Sanctuary (Genesis 28:16-19, 35:7)
____ El Elyon	Most high God, strongest of the strong, Omnipotent, all-powerful God (Genesis 14:18-20)
____ El Olam	Everlasting God (Psalm 90:1-2)
____ Elroi	God who sees, Omniscient, all-knowing God (Genesis 16:13) Omnipresent, God is everywhere (Psalm 139:7-12)
____ El Shaddai	All-sufficient, almighty God (Genesis 17:1)
____ Immanuel	God with us (Isaiah 7:14)
____ Jehovah Jirah	Our Provider (Genesis 22:8, 14)
____ Jehovah M'Kaddesh	Our Sanctification (Leviticus 20:8)
____ Jehovah Nissi	Our Banner of Victory (Exodus 17:15)
____ Jehovah Rohi	Our Good Shepherd (Psalm 23)
____ Jehovah Rophe	Our Healer (Exodus 15:26)
____ Jehovah Sabaoth	The LORD of hosts (Isaiah 6:3)
____ Jehovah Shalom	Our Peace (Judges 6:24)
____ Jehovah Shammah	Ever-present God who is there (Ezekiel 48:35)
____ Jehovah Tsidkenu	Our Righteousness (Jeremiah 23:6)
____ Yahweh	"I Am" (Exodus 3:14)

After the Lord reveals the names you are to pray back to Him, pray aloud the following prayer incorporating several of the names of God:

> ### ❖ Dear Heavenly Father ❖
>
> I am eager to worship You now and cry out like the angels, *"Holy, holy, holy is the LORD of hosts; the whole earth is full of his glory"* (Isaiah 6:3). I proclaim that You are (insert the names of God) and "That the name of the *LORD* is a strong tower; the righteous run into it and are safe. (Proverbs 18:10). In Jesus' name I pray, Amen.

At the beginning of His earthly ministry, Jesus spent forty days in the wilderness fasting. Then, He was tempted by Satan. The devil took Jesus to a very high mountain and showed Him all the kingdoms of the world and their glory. *"'All this I will give you', he said, 'if you will bow down and worship me.' Then Jesus said to him, 'Be gone, Satan! For it is written: You shall worship the Lord your God, and him only shall you serve'"* (Matthew 4:8-10). Jesus was referring to Deuteronomy 6:14-15, which says, *"You shall not go after other gods, the gods of the peoples who are around you — for the LORD your God in your midst is a jealous God...."*

What, in life, is most significant and special to you? Anytime our love, devotion, and trust fall upon another person or thing, we have set up a false god or object of worship. Our adoration and praise are to be directed toward God alone. Jesus said to the woman at the well, *"But the hour is coming, and is now here, when the true worshipers will worship the Father in spirit and truth, for the Father is seeking such people to worship him. God is spirit, and those who worship him must worship in spirit and truth"* (John 4:23-24). The English word for "worship" used to be spelled "worthship" and meant to acknowledge the worth of the object worshiped. We are to recognize God's immeasurable worth in spirit rather than in some material display; in truth rather than in deception.

The Bible says, *"Flee from idolatry"* (1 Corinthians 10:14). Idolatry is setting up a false god or object of worship. An idol could be a person, money, prized possession, hero, athlete, or star. It might even be an ambition or ministry. If your relationship with God takes second place to any person or thing, renounce those false objects of worship and direct all your adoration and worship toward God alone. Jesus said, *"Love the Lord your God with all your heart and with all your soul and with all your mind. This is the first and greatest commandment"* (Matthew 22:37-38).

Use the following prayer to express your commitment and desire to worship God and God alone.

❖ Dear Heavenly Father ❖

Hallowed be Your name. I confess I have allowed other people and things to become more important to me than my personal relationship with You. I have not given You the time and worship that You are worthy of, as my one and only God. I confess that I have not loved You with all my heart, soul and mind (Matthew 22:37-38). I have allowed idols into my life. Lord, I know that any idol in my heart dishonors Your holiness and hurts Your heart. I choose to turn away from my idols, big and small, and to center my life around You alone. I declare that You are my first love (Revelation 2:4-5). Please reveal to my mind any and all idols in my life. In Jesus name I pray, Amen.

The following checklist may help you identify idols you have allowed into your mind or life. Be prepared to renounce anything that has become more important to you than God or that has hurt your relationship with God. Notice that areas listed below are not evil in themselves; they only become wrong when they take over God's rightful place as Lord of your life.

_____ Time

_____ Spouse, children, parents

_____ Relationships, boyfriend, girlfriend, friends

_____ Computer, games

_____ Self, appearance, image, online identity, personal avatars, social media

_____ Ministry, church activities

_____ Occupation, career, position

_____ Sports or talents

_____ Leisure time, pleasure, fun

_____ Hobbies

_____ Comfort, calm, private time

_____ Busyness, activity

_____ Wealth, property, belongings, financial security

_____ Ambition, power, control

_____ Food, drugs, alcohol or substance

_____ Knowledge, degrees

_____ Rockstars, celebrities, athletes

_____ Trophies, medals, honors

_____ Entertainment, TV, movies, music

_____ Popularity, fame, recognition

_____ Worship itself (honoring the pageantry and display rather than God Himself)

_____ The Bible itself (having such a high view of Scripture that you actually worship the book rather than the One the book is written about — see John 5:29-40)

_____ Others _____

Use the following prayer as a guide to help you renounce every idol or wrong priority the Holy Spirit reveals to your mind:

> ### ❖ Dear Heavenly Father ❖
>
> I confess that I have dishonored You by making (person or thing) more important than You. I renounce putting this first in my life as false worship. I choose to have You, Lord, as my first love, with all my heart, soul and mind, and I choose to worship You in Spirit and in truth. In Jesus' name I pray, Amen.

Social Media and the Internet have become such a large part of our daily lives, it's easy to lose our sense of balance. If you have taken your eyes off of Jesus and given too much attention to the things of this world, you may need to pray the following prayer.

> ### ❖ Dear Heavenly Father ❖
>
> Dear heavenly Father, I confess that I have misused my cell phone, the internet and social media to escape reality or as a way of coping with difficult problems. I confess and renounce any way in which I have prioritized online activity over personal relationships. I confess and renounce every way in which I have misrepresented myself online to receive the acceptance others, or to feel better about myself. I choose to find my true identity and full acceptance in You. I repent of receiving worldly philosophies and teachings through the internet. You, Your Word, and the Holy Spirit alone renew my mind and guide me into all truth. I have depended upon apps and social media to bring fulfillment to my life, but now I renounce and break this dependency in the name of Jesus. Only You can meet my deepest needs. I receive your forgiveness and proclaim that You alone give me everything I need for life and godliness (2 Peter 1:3). In Jesus's name I pray, Amen.

God is holy! And you have been made holy and blameless through the blood of Christ (Ephesians 1:4). Part of the Lord's Prayer is to encourage you that you are now His child, and He has declared you holy. Until now, your sense of personal worth may have been determined by what your family, friends, authority figures, or others might have thought of you. Or perhaps a moral failure has left a mark on your mind that seems to say, "I'm no good, I'm just a sinner, I will never amount to anything for God." Those are lies, possibly placed in your mind by the accuser of the brethren (Revelation 12:10).

The truth is that you are in Christ and He is in you. The truth is that in Jesus, you are now acceptable to God. The sinful person you once were is dead, and sin no longer rules in your life (Romans 6:1-6). In contrast, you have been made spiritually alive and have been raised up and seated with Christ in heaven (Ephesians 2:5-6). Nothing is more freeing than agreeing with God about how He sees you and how He feels about you. You must understand what you have in Him and what you can do through Him. Start by filling your mind with the truth from God's word about your acceptance, security, and significance in Christ.

Read these statements that summarize our scriptural identity and position in Christ aloud to proclaim your true identity as God's child and heir.

WHO I AM IN CHRIST

I AM ACCEPTED

- ❖ I am a child of God (John 1:12)
- ❖ I am Jesus' chosen friend (John 15:15)
- ❖ I am holy, accepted, and justified by God (Romans 5:1)
- ❖ I am united to the Lord (1 Corinthians 6:17)
- ❖ I have been bought with a price (1 Corinthians 6:19, 20)
- ❖ I am a part of Christ's family (1 Corinthians 12:27)
- ❖ I am a saint, a holy one (Ephesians 1:1)
- ❖ I have been adopted as God's child (Ephesians 1:5)
- ❖ I have been forgiven and redeemed (Colossians 1:14)
- ❖ I am complete in Christ (Colossians 2:10)

I AM SECURE

- ❖ I am free forever from punishment (Romans 8:1-2)

- ❖ I am sure God works all things for good (Romans 8:28)

- ❖ I am free from condemning charges (Romans 8:31-32)

- ❖ I can't be separated from God's love (Romans 8:35-36)

- ❖ I am hidden with Christ in God (Colossians 3:3)

- ❖ I am sure God will finish His good work (Philippians 1:6)

- ❖ I am a citizen of heaven (Ephesians 2:19)

- ❖ I can find grace and mercy (Hebrews 4:16)

- ❖ I am God's. The evil one cannot touch me (1 John 5:18)

I AM SIGNIFICANT

- ❖ I am salt and light for those near me (Matthew 5:13-14)

- ❖ I am part of the true vine, joined to Christ, and able to produce lots of fruit (John 15:1-5)

- ❖ I am handpicked by Jesus to bear fruit (John 15:16)

- ❖ I am a Spirit-empowered witness of Christ (Acts 1:8)

- ❖ I am a temple of the Holy Spirit (1 Corinthians 3:16)

- ❖ I am at peace with God, and He has given me the work of making peace between Himself and other people (2 Corinthians 5:17-18)

- ❖ I am God's co-worker (2 Corinthians 6:1)

- ❖ I am seated with Christ in heaven (Ephesians 2:6)

- ❖ I am God's building project, His handiwork, created to do His work (Ephesians 2:10)

- ❖ I am able to do all things through Christ, who gives me strength (Philippians 4:13)

Anderson, N.T. & Park, D (2007). Who am I? In *Stomping out the Darkness* (pp 26-28). Bloomington MN: Bethany House Publishers

** You may want to repeat this list for the next 40 days or whenever you feel under spiritual attack.

The Proper Worship of God

It is your responsibility to destroy any false identity equations in your life and replace them with the truth of who you are in Christ. Only you can believe and receive from Him, the truth about who you are in Christ. No one can do it for you. Prayerfully consider the following 12 Identity Indicators below. Mark any areas the Spirit reveals are a struggle for you and then pray the following prayer.

WITHOUT Christ we experience:

Rejection (Ephesians 2:1-3)

Alienation (Ephesians 4:18)

Meaninglessness (Ecclesiastes 1:2)

Weakness (Psalm 27:1)

Timidity (2 Timothy 1:7)

Rebellion (1 Timothy 1:9)

Worry (1 Timothy 1:9)

Being lost (Hebrews 5:11-14)

Fear (Matthew 10:26-33, 2 Timothy 1:7)

Inferiority (Romans 8:37)

Confusion (1 Corinthians 14:33)

Bondage (1 John 4:4)

IN Christ we experience:

Acceptance (Romans 5:1,8,15,17)

Belonging (1 Corinthians 6:17)

Purpose (2 Corinthians 5:17, Colossians 3:4)

Power (Philippians4:18)

Authority (Acts 1:8)

Submission (Romans 13:1-2)

Provision (Philippians 4:19)

Guidance (Romans 8:14)

Security (Romans 8:1,2,28,31)

Significance (John 15:1,5)

Peace (Galatians 5:22)

Freedom (Galatians 5:1)

❖ Dear Heavenly Father ❖

Thank You for making me a new creation in Christ and a saint, a holy person (Ephesians 1:1). I understand that I am now a member of a chosen race, a royal priesthood, a holy nation (1 Peter 2:9,10). I confess that I have not always believed what You said about me and that I have let personal events or people determine my identity. I specifically renounce the lie that I am _____ or my struggle with_____ and I announce that in Christ I have _____. Jesus is the true source of identity and meaning, so I renounce my old identity and embrace my new identity in Christ. In Jesus' name I pray, Amen.

New Life Brings New Identity

Being a Christian is not just about getting something; it's about being someone. A Christian is not merely a person who gets forgiven, gets to go to heaven, gets the Holy Spirit, or gets a new nature. In terms of our deepest identity, a Christian is a saint, a holy one, a spiritually born child of God, a divine masterpiece, a child of light, a citizen of heaven. Being born again changed you into someone who didn't exist before. What you get from God isn't the point; The point is who you are. It's not what you do as a Christian that determines who you are; it's who you are that determines what you do (check out 2 Corinthians 5:17, Ephesians 2:10, 1 Peter 2:9-10, 1 John 3:1-2).

"Your kingdom come"

God is the king and supreme ruler of all things. That's why we call Him our sovereign Lord (Ephesians 1). He is also eternal, meaning He and His kingdom will never end (Psalm 90:2). When you pray, "Your kingdom come," you're inviting God to rule in your heart intimately and expressing your willingness to follow His will and ways. You are eager to make His kingdom internal and personal. God is your mighty king, and you are His subject. You are asking God to rule in your heart, just as He now rules in heaven, and are submitting to His kingdom plans. We are still imperfect people, and God's rule in our lives is not complete, but thankfully we model growth, not perfection. God's holy standard is still there, however, and He desires to rule in you today.

Unfortunately, rebellion may occur. It is impossible to live fully for God's kingdom if you rebel against God and those He has placed in authority over you (Romans 13:1-7). Submission and a heart of surrender and trust show God that you desire to live for His kingdom rather than living for self and your purposes. Sometimes we ask God to bless our plan or ministry rather than seeking to join God in His. Even this is a subtle form of rebellion. God wants more than just an outward form of submission in your life. He wants your heart to submit to Him, and His kingdom plans in every way. Rebellion makes you a wide-open target for the enemy. You will never be able to resist the devil and have him leave you alone until you first submit to God (James 4:7). Submission is an act of surrender. To commit yourself to living for God's kingdom and to a lifestyle of submission and surrender to God, pray the following prayer aloud:

❖ Dear Heavenly Father ❖

I pray "Your kingdom come" first and foremost in my heart and life. I want to live for Your Kingdom. I confess that at times I have rebelled against You and Your Kingdom work. You have said in Your word that rebellion is the same thing as witchcraft, and being self-willed is like serving false gods (1 Samuel 15:23). I know that my thoughts and actions have defied You, and that I have rebelled against You and those You have placed in authority over me. I have rejected Your leadership and protection. I thank You for forgiving my rebellion. I choose to submit to You and Your ways. I resist the devil and his ways and close any doors I may have opened through my rebellion. Please show me now all the ways I have rebelled against You, Father, and those You have placed in authority over me. In Jesus' name I pray, Amen.

At times those in authority may abuse their power over you. In those cases, do not give up on authority, but rather go to a higher authority to get help. For example, God is not asking a wife to submit to a physically abusive husband. Physical, mental, emotional, or sexual abuse by authorities is not part of God's plan. Report all abuse to the law or protective agencies. If a person in authority asked you to break God's law or compromise your commitment, you need to obey God rather than man (Acts 4:19, 20).

We are told to submit to one another as equals in Christ (Ephesians 5:21). However, God uses specific lines of authority to protect and provide for us the safety and security we need. He uses this to bring order to our daily lives.

Examine each of the areas of authority listed below and ask the Lord to reveal to you any specific ways you have not respected these positions or submitted to them:

_____ **God**
His guidance, His Lordship, surrendering to His will for your life (Daniel 9:5, 9).

_____ **Church leaders**
Pastor, youth pastor, Sunday school teacher (Hebrews 13:7).

_____**Employers, Educators**
Boss, supervisor (1 Peter 2:18-23), teachers, coaches, school officials (Romans 13:1-4).

_____ **Civil Government**
Tax laws, traffic laws, attitude toward government or officials (Romans 13:1-7, 1 Timothy 2:1-4, 1 Peter 2:13-17).

_____ **Family**
Husband or Wife (1 Peter 3:1-4 and Ephesians 5:21, 1 Peter 3:7), parents, step-parents, legal guardians (Ephesians 6:1-3).

For each area of rebellion the Lord shows you, pray the following prayer aloud:

❖ Dear Heavenly Father ❖

I agree with You that I have rebelled against _____. Thank you for forgiving and removing my rebellion. I choose to submit to You and Your leadership and protection as well as those You have placed over me. In Jesus' name I pray, Amen.

Living for God's kingdom means being under authority, but it also means that you have been given a measure of authority. Jesus said, "…*all authority in heaven and on earth has been given to me"* (Matthew 28:18). He was given all authority as a result of His death and resurrection (Ephesians 1:18-21). Jesus took His rightful place at the Father's side, the right hand of God, the position of all authority and power (Ephesians 1:20-21, Hebrews 1:3). Jesus' authority extends over everyone and everything for all time, not only while He was here on earth; but also in the age to come (Ephesians 1:20-21, 1 Corinthians 15:24-28). Because you have accepted Christ as your Savior, you have been placed in Christ and raised up with Him and are now seated with Him at the right hand of God (Ephesians 2:6). You now share Christ's seat of authority. Because you are under the authority of Christ, the devil must leave you alone when you stand firm and resist him (James 4:7). Some Christians struggle in their spiritual walk because they fail to assert the authority they have in Christ. Jesus warns us not to boast about our authority over Satan, but rather to rejoice that we are safe in Christ and will spend eternity with Him (Luke 10:20). Also, we are never to use our authority in Christ as an excuse to push others around. We are to serve others (Ephesians 5:21, Matthew 20:25-28, Mark 10:45).

You will have authority and power as long as you are submitted to Christ. Nowhere in the Bible are we told to pray for power but rather to submit to Christ. When you submit to Christ, you have all the power and authority you need to stand against the world, the flesh, and the devil. Use the following prayer to express your authority in Christ:

❖ Dear Heavenly Father ❖

I confess at times I have been passive; I have failed to claim the incredible authority that is mine in Christ. I choose to be strong in the Lord and the strength of His might (Ephesians 6:10). I choose to walk according to my new identity in Christ and be filled with the Spirit, by depending on His mighty power alone rather than my own strength. And I know that when I do submit to God and resist the devil, that he has to flee from me (James 4:7). I choose therefore to take up the full armor of God, that I may be able to resist in the day of evil (Ephesians 6:13). In Jesus' name I pray, Amen.

"Your will be done on earth as it is in heaven"

"When you pray, "Your will be done on earth as it is in heaven," you are confessing that the way you live here on earth is often different than how you would live if you were right now in heaven with God. God's holy angels don't pray about doing His will; they just do it. In heaven, God's plans are followed instantly and perfectly, not later, when it is more convenient or fits into one's schedule. In heaven, God's will is done completely, not to some extent or partially. What are you seeking when you pray for the will of God?

First, that you would know God's personal plan for your life.

Secondly, that you would trust the decision making ability of God. He does have a plan for your life. Jeremiah 29:11 says, *"For I know the plans that I have for you, declares the LORD, plans for welfare, and not for evil, to give you a future and a hope."* You are to ask God for His blueprint for your life and trust that God will make the right decisions for your life. These two things are absolutely necessary if you desire to have God's will done here on earth as it is in heaven.

We do not ask God to change His will; He can't change His character or who He is (James 1:17). It is not our role to direct His will, for He alone is the sovereign ruler of all things, and He is independent of His creation (Isaiah 40:13-14). We do not ask God to bless our will; God can only bless those choices consistent with who He is and His attributes (1 John 5:14).

We are being instructed in the Lord's Prayer to ask God to help us recognize and do His will. God has a plan for your life, and it is your responsibility to seek God and discover His perfect will. God may not reveal every part of His will to you at this time. If He did, you would be overwhelmed. That is why we are to pray often, "Your will be done on earth as it is in heaven." But you are responsible for what He has shown you today. Pray this prayer aloud as a guide to help you discover God's will for your life.

❖ Dear Heavenly Father ❖

Your word says if any of you lacks wisdom, you should ask God who gives generously to all (James 1:5-6). Your word also says that you speak to me by the Holy Spirit who dwells within me (1 Corinthians 2:11-12). I trust you completely and understand that you always lead me to righteousness. I ask you for wisdom and leading to know and follow your divine plan for my life, today and into the future. I choose to listen to your voice and do what you ask me to. I pray all this in Jesus' name, Amen.

Write down what you sense Him saying to you today about His divine will for your life.

Use the following prayer to proclaim your trust in God and the plan He has revealed to you:

❖ Dear Heavenly Father ❖

I confess that I have often been the controller of my own thinking. But I belong to You. Lord, I choose now to adopt Your plans for my life, specifically (what He revealed today). I choose to trust You completely and follow You and Your plans for my life in the power of the Holy Spirit. In Jesus' name I pray, Amen.

"Give us this day our daily bread"

God, your "Abba" Father, loves you and wants to provide for all your needs, both spiritually and physically. The word "bread" is used as a symbol. It can stand for food, as we most commonly think of it, or it could be money, time, work, etc. Bread is the required provision to meet your daily needs. When you pray, "Give us this day our daily bread," you are recognizing God the Father as the one who provides you with the things you need to survive.

First, you need to acknowledge that you have needs.

Second, put your trust in God to supply your needs.

Third, you must ask God to supply your needs.

Fourth, you must understand that God is going to supply your needs daily—not monthly or yearly—but day by day.

Jesus said, *"Ask, and it will be given to you; seek, and you will find; knock, and it will be opened to you"* (Matthew 7:7). God does not give us everything we ask for, but He does give us everything we need. Sometimes, however, you have not because you ask not or ask with wrong motives (James 4:2-3).

In addition to asking God to meet your needs, you must also recognize your responsibility to give back to God and demonstrate your thanks to Him. Malachi 3:8 says, *"Will man rob God? Yet you are robbing me. But you say, 'How have we robbed you?' In your tithes and contributions."* And God says, *"Bring the full tithe into the storehouse, that there may be food in my house. And thereby put me to the test, says the LORD of hosts, if I will not open the windows of heaven for you and pour down for you a blessing until there is no more need"* (Malachi 3:10). God wants you to depend on Him and acknowledge Him as Jehovah–Jirah, your provider (Genesis 22:8,14).

The following checklist may help you identify where you are not trusting God for physical and spiritual provision in your life.

_____ I have acted self-sufficiently as if I have no needs (physical, spiritual, emotional, etc.).

_____ I have failed to ask God to meet my needs and turn to Him alone and trust Him.

_____ I have looked to people around me to meet my need for acceptance and belonging.

_____ I have expected God to meet my financial needs all at once, rather than day by day.

_____ I have expected others to meet my need for security rather than God.

_____ I have expected God to meet my desires rather than my needs.

_____ I have sought out a sense of significance from my work or home rather than from God.

_____ I have failed to give back to God my tithe and offerings as I should.

Use the following prayer as a guide to help you renounce your lack of dependence on God, your Father:

❖ Dear Heavenly Father ❖

I ask You to provide for me this day my daily bread. I realize that I have not always acknowledged You as Jehovah-Jirah, my provider. I have depended on myself and my own resources to meet my needs. I specifically renounce that _____.
I choose to depend on You alone Lord. Thank you that you promise to bless me and provide for my daily needs. Give me everything I need to glorify you today. In Jesus' name I pray, Amen.

"And forgive us our debts"

God loves you and wants you to experience His peace as you follow Him. Sometimes, however, you may fail to follow God's will and ways.

The Bible identifies this failure using six keywords: **sin** (Romans 3:23), **debt** (Matthew 6:12), **lawlessness** (1 John 3:4), **transgression** (Psalm 32:5), **trespass** (Ephesians 2:1, Matthew 6:14), and **wickedness** (Psalm 106:6).

Words for sin	Meaning
Debt	What is owed, your obligation, the consequences of your sin
Lawlessness	Open flagrant rejection of God's commands, disrespect for the law
Sin	Missing the mark, inability to do good or display holiness
Transgression	To step across the line, loss of self-control, no restraint
Trespass	A fall or slip, infatuation, passion of the moment
Wickedness	An immoral, depraved or wicked desire, lewdness, unclean, dirty

Jesus is asking you to pray, "Forgive us our debts." He used the word 'debt,' which, in many ways, encompasses all the other words for sin plus seeks release from the punishment of sin. In this petition, you will confess and renounce any past or present area of sin in your life. All your sins were forgiven at the cross, but if you struggle with a habit or stronghold that repeatedly surfaces, confessing and renouncing your sin will close that open door to the enemy.

In order to help you evaluate the spiritual experiences of your life, fill out the checklists under each category of sin. If the list does not include something you have done which you feel should be included, be sure to add it. Even if you were "innocently" involved in something, or only watched someone else who was involved, you should write it on your list and renounce it, in case you gave Satan a foothold without realizing it.

Don't be surprised if you feel some resistance as you complete this petition. Satan doesn't want you to be free, and he will do whatever he can do to keep you from claiming your freedom. Before you go through this petition, pray in the following way:

> ### ❖ Dear Heavenly Father ❖
>
> I ask You to reveal to me anything that I have done or that someone has done to me that is spiritually wrong. Please show me any sin in my life and reveal to my mind if I have been involved with any wrong practices or harmful habits, whether I knew I was involved or not. I want to experience freedom from sin and do Your will. I ask this in Jesus' name, Amen.

Go through the checklist carefully and check any of the following activities you have participated in any way; your sin may fit more than one category. The purpose is not to categorize your sin but to confess and renounce it. Use the categories only as an aid to help you identify what you need to confess and renounce. Proverbs 28:13 NIV says, *"Whoever conceals their sin does not prosper, but the one who confesses and renounces them finds mercy."* Your Father God is ready to hand out all the mercy you need.

Pause after each bold section, and pray the prayer at the end of the checklist. Use the prayer as a guide for confession and renouncing each item checked.

Sin - missing the mark, inability to do good or display holiness

____ Saying I have no sin   ____ Believing I can be holy on my own

Debt - what is owed, your obligation, the punishment of your sin.

____ Greed   ____ Stealing   ____ Other _____

Lawlessness - open, flagrant rejection of God's commands, disrespect for the law.

____ Fighting   ____ Drunkenness   ____ Vandalism   ____ Drugs

____ Disregard for God's laws   ____ Other _____

Transgression - to step across the line, loss of self-control, no restraint.

____ Anger   ____ Lying   ____ Swearing   ____ Insults

____ Rebellion   ____ Perfectionism   ____ Other _____

Trespass - a fall or slip, infatuation, passion of the moment.

____ Lustful thoughts   ____ Lustful actions   ____ Hatred   ____ Envy

____ Gossip   ____ Jealousy   ____ Argumentative

____ Cheating   ____ Coveting   ____ Other _____

Wickedness - an immoral, depraved or wicked desire, lewdness, unclean, and occult activity.

____ Ouija board   ____ Tarot card   ____ Out-of-body experience

____ Bloody Mary   ____ Spirit guides   ____ Magic Eight Ball   ____ Trances

____ Fortune-telling   ____ Palm-reading   ____ Astrology   ____ Aliens

____ Automatic writing   ____ Table lifting   ____ Satanism   ____ Sorcery

____ Hypnosis   ____ Witchcraft   ____ Séances   ____ Seeing ghost

____ Horoscopes   ____ Sexual spirits   ____ Using spells or curses

____ Levitation   ____ Superstitions   ____ Black or White Magic

____ Mental telepathy   ____ Fantasy Games   ____ Dungeons & Dragons

____ Cutting yourself   ____ Blood pacts   ____ Martial arts devotion to sensei

____ Objects of worship, crystals, luck charms   ____ Occult/role play video games

____ Other _____

❖ Dear Heavenly Father ❖

I confess that I have participated in (name each item). Thank You for showing me now how I have acted against You. I ask Your forgiveness, and I renounce this as a counterfeit to true Christianity. Thank you that in Christ I am forgiven, Amen.

After you have confessed and renounced each item, pray the following prayer:

> ### ❖ Dear Heavenly Father ❖
>
> It is Your kindness that has led me to repentance. Thank you for revealing these sins to my mind. I confess that I participated in these sins and that they were offensive to You. I know that my involvement may have opened doors in my life to the enemies of the Lord Jesus Christ, so I confess my sin and close any and all doors that may have been opened by my disobedience to You. I declare that I am forgiven by the blood of Christ and that He alone is the Lord of my life. I thank you for Your forgiveness. In Jesus' name I pray, Amen.

Sexual Sins

Not all sin is the same. Sexual sin is different from other sins, because it involves your body, creating a spiritual bonding. The Bible says, *"Do you not know that your bodies are members of Christ? Shall I then take the members of Christ and make them members of a prostitute? Never! Or do you not know that he who is joined to a prostitute becomes one body with her? For, as it is written, 'The two will become one flesh.' But he who is joined to the Lord becomes one spirit with Him. Flee from sexual immorality. Every other sin a person commits is outside the body, but the sexually immoral person sins against his own body. Or do you not know that your body is a temple of the Holy Spirit within you, whom you have from God? You are not your own, for you were bought with a price. So glorify God in your body"* (1 Corinthians 6:15-20).

The next part of this petition deals with sexuality and sexual sins. If you have been caught in the trap of sin-confess, sin-confess, you may need to follow the suggestion of James 5:16: *"Therefore, confess your sins to one another and pray for one another, that you may be healed. The prayer of a righteous person has great power as it is working."* Find a spiritually mature person who will hold you up in prayer and check up on you from time to time. Others may only need the assurance of 1 John 1:9: *"If we confess our sins, he is faithful and just to forgive us our sins and to cleanse us from all unrighteousness."* It is your responsibility not to allow sin to control you by using your body as an instrument of unrighteousness (Romans 6:12-13).

Ask God to help you identify where you are struggling and to show you where you have been trapped. You may find issues of gender confusion, homosexuality, voyeurism, or deviant sexual behaviors. Or you may identify that you are struggling with habitual sexual sins such as pornography, masturbation, sexual promiscuity, or petting. Whether you need to confess to others or just to God, pray the following prayer:

❖ Dear Heavenly Father ❖

You have said, *"But put on the Lord Jesus Christ, and make no provision for the flesh, to gratify its desires"* (Romans 13:14). I understand that I have given in to fleshly lusts which wage war against my soul (1 Peter 2:11). I thank You that in Christ my sins are forgiven, but I have broken Your holy law and have given the enemy an opportunity to wage war in my body (Romans 6:12-13, 1 Peter 5:8, James 4:1). I come before Your presence to admit these sins and to seek Your cleansing (1 John 1:9) that I may be freed from the bondage of sin. I now ask You to reveal to my mind the ways that I have broken Your moral law and disappointed the Holy Spirit; to reveal to my mind every sexual use of my body as an instrument of unrighteousness. In Jesus' precious name I pray, Amen.

As the Lord brings to your mind every inappropriate sexual use of your body, whether it was done to you (for example, rape, incest, or any sexual molestation) or done willingly by you, renounce every occasion.

> Lord, I renounce (name the specific use of your body) and I break that sinful bond with (name of the person).

Now commit your body to the Lord by praying:

> Lord, I renounce all these uses of my body as an instrument of unrighteousness. I also confess any willful participation. I now present my whole body to You, my eyes, my mouth, my mind, my heart, my hands, my feet and my sexual organs as a living sacrifice, holy and acceptable unto You; and I reserve the sexual use of my body for marriage only (Hebrews 13:4). I renounce the lie of Satan that my body is not clean, that it is dirty or in any way unacceptable as a result of my past sexual experiences. Lord, I thank You that You have totally cleansed and forgiven me, that You love and accept me unconditionally, just as I am. Therefore, I can accept myself and my body as clean in Your eyes. In Jesus' name I pray, Amen.

"I appeal to you therefore, brothers, by the mercies of God, to present your bodies as a living sacrifice, holy and acceptable to God, which is your spiritual worship. Do not be conformed to this world, but be transformed by the renewal of your mind, that by testing you may discern what is the will of God, what is good and acceptable and perfect" (Romans 12:1-2).

Note: For specific help walking through gender confusion issues see Appendix A (p. 125)

"As we forgive our debtors"

In petition six you were forgiven! Now it's time to forgive others who have hurt you. If you do not forgive people who hurt or offend you, it makes you a wide-open target for Satan to attack and take advantage of you (2 Corinthians 2:10-11). Choosing not to forgive opens a door to personal torment and prevents us from fully experiencing God's forgiveness and walking confidently in fellowship with Him (Matthew 18:21-35, Matthew 6:15). This is one of the reasons Jesus included, "as we forgive our debtors," in the Lord's prayer - He wants us to be free from any form of bitterness (Hebrews 12:15). We are to forgive others as God has shown us mercy and forgiveness (Luke 6:36, Ephesians 4:31-32).

Ask God to bring to mind those you need to forgive as you pray this prayer aloud:

❖ Dear Heavenly Father ❖

Thank You for Your kindness and patience which led me to turn from my sin (Romans 2:4). I have not always been kind, patient, and loving toward others, especially those who have hurt me. I have been bitter and resentful. I give You my emotions, and ask You to bring to mind all my painful memories so I can choose to forgive from my heart. I ask You to bring to my mind the people I need to forgive (Matthew 18:35). I ask this in the precious name of Jesus, who will heal me from my hurts, Amen.

On a sheet of paper, or in this section, make a list of the names which come to mind. Don't be surprised if your parents are near the top. In 90 percent of the people we lead through these petitions, the first two names on the list are their parents. The two most often overlooked names on the lists are self and God. Forgiving yourself for your failures shows that you accept God's cleansing and forgiveness. Technically, we don't need to forgive God. He certainly hasn't done anything wrong—He can't. But maybe you cried out to Him with a need, and He didn't seem to answer, so you are angry with Him. You may need to release Him for not living up to your false expectations.

If you need to, look back at petition one to make sure you have no thoughts against God.

Before you pray to forgive the people on your list, here are a few important things you need to understand about forgiveness:

❖ Forgiveness is not forgetting. People who try to forget the pain caused by others often find they cannot. God says He will remember our sins no more (Hebrews 10:17). But God knows everything, and He can't forget. "Remember our sins no more" means that God will never use our sins against us (Psalm 103:12). You may not be able to forget your past, but you can be free from it. When we bring up the past and use it against others, we haven't forgiven them.

❖ Forgiveness is a choice. We may feel that it's impossible to forgive someone. But since God requires us to forgive, it is something we can do. God would never require us to do something we cannot do. We forgive by choosing to forgive.

❖ Forgiveness means giving up on revenge. Forgiveness is not justifying the act of injustice or saying we weren't hurt or wounded. It is choosing to release the offender from paying the debt owed to us. We are told never to take our own revenge (Romans 12:19). "Why should I let them off the hook?" we argue. When we forgive, we let them off *our* hook, but they aren't off *God's* hook. He will deal with them fairly — something we can't do.

❖ If we don't let the offenders off our hook, we are bound to them and our hurts. We can stop the pain by forgiving. We don't forgive someone just for their sake; we do it for ourselves, so we can be free. Your need to forgive isn't an issue between you and the person who hurt you; it's between you and God.

❖ Forgiveness is agreeing to live with the consequences of another person's sin. It costs us something to forgive. We pay a price for the hurt we forgive. We are going to live with the consequences whether we want to or not. Our only choice is whether we will do so in the bondage of bitterness or the freedom of forgiveness.

How do we forgive from our heart? First, we must admit the hurt, pain, or hatred we feel, instead of burying them deep inside. If forgiveness doesn't include our emotions, it will be incomplete. You may not know how to deal with your feelings, but God does. Let Him bring the pain to the surface so He can deal with it. This is where healing begins.

Forgiveness doesn't mean that you have to put up with continuing sin. It is possible to forgive the sins of the past and take a stand against the sins of the present. Don't wait to forgive until you feel like forgiving. You will never get there. Feelings will take time to heal after the choice to forgive is made, and Satan has lost his place (Ephesians 4:26,27).

For each person on your list, pray aloud:

> Lord, I choose to forgive (name the person) for (specifically name all his or her offenses and the painful memories that come to your mind), which made me feel (share painful feelings). Lord, You forgive me, so I choose to forgive (name the person).

Keep praying about each person until you are sure that you have dealt with all the pain you remember. Positive feelings will follow in time; freeing yourself from the hurts of the past is the important issue. After you have forgiven each person on your list, finish this petition by praying aloud:

❖ Dear Heavenly Father ❖

I choose to uproot any bitterness in my life and to release any resentment I have toward others. I thank You for setting me free from my bondage to bitterness. I surrender my right to seek revenge and ask You to heal my damaged emotions. I choose to be like Christ and forgive my debtors. I now ask you to bless those who hurt me. In Jesus' name I pray, Amen.

"And do not lead us into temptation"

The Bible warns us to be on the alert and to make sure our minds are clear. You can be tempted at any time (1 Corinthians 10:13). When you ask God to "lead you not into temptation," you are asking your Father to guide your steps along the pathways He would travel. It is refusing to travel down the paths of the world, the flesh, and the devil. You are letting God take control and depending on His word and Spirit to reveal His moral ways. A Christian is never above being tempted or deceived by the 'father of lies' (John 8:44). The devil accuses us day and night (Revelation 12:10).

The previous petitions focused on past sin, while this petition, "Lead us not into temptation," focuses on future sins. You can only spot the darkness of deception in the light of truth. Jesus is the truth, and the truth is found in the Bible, God's word. God desires us to plant His truth in our hearts so we can say "no" to sin (Psalm 51:6).

When David lived a lie, he suffered. When he finally found freedom by agreeing with the truth, he wrote, *"Blessed is the man... in whose spirit there is no deceit"* (Psalm 32:2). We must get rid of anything false in our lives and speak the truth in love (Ephesians 4:15, 25). Begin this petition by breaking the entrenched patterns that lead to saying yes to temptation by reading aloud the following prayer:

❖ Dear Heavenly Father ❖

I know that when I am tempted, it often looks like the truth, but it is really a lie wrapped in a tiny truth. I want to know You and Your word so well that when I see even a hint of a lie I can expose it and turn from it. I know that if I say "no" to temptation and choose to believe the truth, I will always walk free (John 8:32).

I confess that I have not always said "no" to temptation and I have believed lies. I have been deceived by Satan, the father of lies (John 8:44), and I have deceived myself (1 John 1:8). I thought I could hide it from You, but You see everything and still love me. I am Your child through the death, burial, and resurrection of my Lord, Jesus Christ. Therefore, by the authority of the Lord Jesus Christ, I command all evil spirits to leave me. I ask the Holy Spirit to lead me into all truth. I ask You, Father, to look deep inside me and know my heart. Show me if there is anything in me that I am trying to hide (Psalm 139:23-24), so I can resist any temptation that comes my way and walk free. In Jesus' name I pray, Amen.

Take some time at this point to think of the evil tricks Satan has used to deceive you. Have you been listening to false teachers or deceiving spirits? Have you been living under self-deception? Have you used excuses to defend your behavior? Now that you are alive in Christ and forgiven, you don't have to live a lie or defend yourself! Check those below that apply to you:

Ways I Can Be Deceived By The World

_____ Believing that I can say "yes" to temptation and sin without it affecting me, others, or my fellowship with God (Revelation 3:20, Hebrews 3:12-13).

_____ Believing that there are no consequences on earth for saying "yes" to temptation and sin (Galatians 6:7-8).

_____ Believing that God will take all the fun out of my life if I say "no" to temptation (John 10:10).

_____ Believing that I need more than what God has given me in Christ (2 Corinthians 11:2-4; 13-15).

_____ Believing that I can read, see or listen to anything I want and not be spiritually affected (Proverbs 4:23-27; 6:27-28, Matthew 5:28).

_____ Believing that I can associate with bad company and not become distorted in my beliefs and actions (1 Corinthians 15:33-34, Proverbs 1:8-10; 4:14-15).

_____ Believing that money and things will bring contentment (Matthew 13:22, 1 Timothy 6:10).

_____ Believing that excessive food or alcohol can make me happy or take away my stress (Proverbs 20:1; 23:19-21).

_____ Believing that an attractive or sexy body will get me what I want or need (Proverbs 31:30, 1 Peter 3:3-4).

_____ Others_____

Lord, I agree that I have been deceived in the area of _____.
Thank You for forgiving me. I commit myself to know and follow Your truth.

Ways I Can Deceive Myself

_____ Hearing God's word but not doing what it says (James 1:22; 4:17).

_____ Saying I have no sin (1 John 1:8).

_____ Thinking I am something I am not (Galatians 6:3).

_____ Thinking I am wise in the things of the world (1 Corinthians 3:18,19).

_____ Thinking I will not reap what I sow (Galatians 6:7).

_____ Thinking that the unrighteous people will share in God's kingdom (1 Corinthians 6:9).

_____ Thinking I can be a good Christian and still hurt others by what I say (James 1:26).

Lord, I agree that I have deceived myself in the area of_____.
Thank You for forgiving me. I commit myself to know and follow Your truth.

Wrong Ways To Defend Myself

_____ Refusing to face the real things that have happened to you (denial of reality).

_____ Escaping from the real world, fantasy life.

_____ Withdrawing to avoid rejection, emotional insulation.

_____ Reverting to a less threatening time (regression).

_____ Taking out frustrations on others (displaced anger).

_____ Blaming others (projection).

_____ Looking for an excuse (rationalization).

_____ Misrepresenting myself, creating a phony image (deception).

Lord, I agree that I have tried to defend myself by _____.
Thank You for forgiving me. I commit myself to know and follow Your truth.

Choosing truth and saying "no" to temptation may be difficult if you have been living a lie (being deceived) for some time. Knowing that you are forgiven and accepted as God's child is what sets you free to face reality and declare your dependence on Him.

When you pray, "Lead me not into temptation," you are not praying, "Lord, don't tempt me," because God will never tempt you. James 1:13 says, *"Let no one say when he is tempted, 'I am being tempted by God,' for God cannot be tempted with evil, and he Himself tempts no one."*

In the same way, when you pray, "Lead me not into temptation" you are not praying, "Don't allow me to be tempted." That kind of prayer denies the reality of the world, the flesh, and the devil. Facing and resisting temptation develops our faith. Truth is God's way of responding to temptation, and faith is God's way for us to respond to the truth. Believing the truth is a choice. When someone says, "I want to believe God, but I just can't," they are being deceived. Of course, we can believe God! Acting in faith is something you decide to do, not just something you feel like doing. Believing the truth doesn't make it true. It's true, so we believe it.

Embracing Humility

Pride is a killer. Pride says, "I can do it! I can get myself out of this mess without God's or anyone else's help." Oh no we can't! We absolutely need God, and we desperately need each other! Paul wrote: *"We...worship by the Spirit of God and glory in Christ Jesus and put no confidence in the flesh"* (Philippians 3:3).

Humility is confidence properly placed in God. We are to *"be strong in the Lord, and in the strength of His might"* (Ephesians 6:10). In fact, James 4:6-10 and 1 Peter 5:1-10 tell us that spiritual problems will follow when we are proud.

Ask God to show you any specific areas in your life where you have been prideful. Check those which apply to you:

_____ I have a stronger desire to do my will than God's will.

_____ I rely on my own strength rather than God's.

_____ Too often I think my ideas are better than others'.

_____ I want to control others rather than develop self-control.

_____ Sometimes I consider myself more important than others.

_____ Sometimes I find it difficult to admit I was wrong.

_____ I am often a people-pleaser instead of a God-pleaser.

_____ I am overly concerned about getting the credit I deserve.

_____ I often think I am more humble than others.

_____ I often believe I am smarter than those in authority over me (parents, boss, teachers, etc.).

_____ I often feel my needs are more important than the needs of others.

_____ Other_____

Lord, I agree that I have been prideful in the area of _____.
Please forgive me for my pride. I choose to humble myself and place all my
confidence in You. In Jesus' name I pray, Amen.

Use the following prayer to express your commitment to living humbly before God:

❖ Dear Heavenly Father ❖

You have said that pride goes before destruction and an arrogant spirit before
stumbling (Proverbs 16:18). I confess that I have been thinking mainly of myself and
not of others. I have not denied myself, picked up my cross daily, and followed You
(Matthew 16:24). I have believed that I am the only one who cares about me, so I must
take care of myself. I have turned away from You and have not let You love me.

I am tired of living for myself and by myself. I now confess that I have sinned against
You by placing my will before Yours and by centering my life around self instead of
You. I renounce my pride and selfishness. I cancel any ground gained by the enemies
of the Lord Jesus Christ. I ask You to fill me with Your Holy Spirit so I can do Your will.

I give my heart to You and stand against all the ways that Satan attacks me. I ask You
to show me how to live for others. I now choose to regard others as more important
than myself and to make You the most important of all (Phil. 2 :3-11 Romans 12:10).
I ask this in the name of Christ Jesus my Lord, Amen.

"But deliver us from the evil one."

When you pray, "deliver us from the evil one," you are agreeing that you believe in someone supremely evil. The Bible identifies him as Satan, and his agenda is not to simply trifle with believers but to steal, kill, and destroy them. He will do whatever he can to harm you. When you pray, "deliver us from evil," you are admitting that life is a spiritual struggle with a spiritual enemy that opposes you and God. *"For our struggle is not against flesh and blood, but against the rulers, against the authorities, against the powers of this dark world and against the spiritual forces of evil in the heavenly realms"* (Ephesians 6:12).

Ask God to reveal to your mind any activities or spiritual experiences you have been involved in as you read through the questions on the next page. These questions will help you identify any non-Christian practices you have been involved in. Even if you were "innocently" involved in something, or only watching someone else who was involved, you should write it down and renounce it, in case you gave Satan a foothold without realizing it. If the Holy Spirit brings it to your mind, then act on it.

Don't be surprised if you feel some resistance as you complete this petition. Satan doesn't want you to be free, and he will do everything he can to keep you from claiming your freedom.

As you go through this petition, pray in the following way:

❖ Dear Heavenly Father ❖

I ask You to reveal to me anything that I have done or that someone has done to me that is spiritually wrong. Show me any sin in my life. Please reveal to my mind if I have been involved with any cults, false religions, occult/satanic practices or false teachers, whether I knew I was involved or not. I want to experience freedom from sin and do Your will. I ask this in Jesus' name, Amen.

____ Have you ever suffered sleep paralysis?

____ Have you ever been involved in non-Christian religions (Islam, Buddhism, Hinduism, etc.)?

____ Have you ever had non-Christian spiritual experiences through cults (Mormonism, Christian Science, Jehovah's Witnesses, etc.)?

____ Have you ever been involved in a secret brotherhood or society (Masons, Sorority/Fraternity, etc.)?

____ Have you ever been involved in mind-influencing activities (Yoga, TM, Hypnosis, etc.)?

____ Have you been involved in any type of media (movies, TV, music, books, magazines, comic books, video/role-playing games, etc.) which may have influenced you negatively, caused fear or nightmares, glorified Satan, violence, or things of a sexual or fleshly nature?

____ Have you ever felt, heard, or seen a spiritual being in your room?

____ Have you ever had a reoccurring nightmare?

____ Have you ever had an imaginary friend who talks to you?

____ Have you ever heard voices in your head or had repeating, nagging thoughts like, "I'm dumb," "I'm ugly," "I can't do anything right," etc., as if there were a conversation going on in your head?

____ Have you or anyone in your family ever consulted a medium, spiritist, or channeler?

____ What other spiritual experiences have you had that could be considered out of the ordinary (telepathy, speaking in a trance, knowing something supernaturally, etc.)?

____ Have you ever been involved in satanic worship of any form or attended a concert where Satan was the focus? Have you ever been involved in satanic rituals or heavy occult activity?

When you are sure that your list is complete, confess and renounce each involvement by praying aloud the following prayer, repeating it separately for each item on your list.

❖ Dear Heavenly Father ❖

I confess that I have participated in _____. I renounce this as a counterfeit to true Christianity. I know this is wrong and I ask for Your forgiveness.

After you have confessed and renounced each item, pray the following prayer:

❖ Dear Heavenly Father ❖

It is Your kindness that has led me to repentance. Thank You for revealing these sins to my mind. I confess that I did participate in these sins and that they were offensive to You. I know that my involvement may have opened doors in my life to the enemies of the Lord Jesus Christ, so I confess my sin and close any and all doors that may have been opened by my disobedience to You. I declare that I am forgiven by the blood of Christ and that He alone is the Lord of my life. I thank You for Your forgiveness. In Jesus' name I pray, Amen.

Overcoming Fear

One of the major weapons of the evil one is fear. 1 Peter 5:8 says that our enemy, the devil, prowls around like a roaring lion, seeking people to devour. Just as a lion's roar strikes terror into the hearts of those who hear it, so Satan uses fear to try and paralyze Christians. His intimidation tactics are designed to rob us of faith in God and drive us to try and get our needs met through the world or the flesh.

Fear frightens us, causes us to be self-centered, and clouds our minds so that all we can think about is the thing that frightens us. But fear can only control us if we let it.

However, God does not want us to be mastered by anything, including fear (1 Corinthians 6:12). Jesus Christ is to be our only master (2 Timothy 2:21, John 13:13). To begin to experience freedom from the bondage of fear and be able to walk by faith in God, pray the following prayer from your heart:

❖ Dear Heavenly Father ❖

I confess to You that I have listened to the devil's roar and have allowed fear to master me. I have not always walked by faith, but instead have focused on my feelings and circumstances (2 Corinthians 4:16-18; 5:7). I thank You for forgiving me for my unbelief. Right now I renounce the spirit of fear and affirm the truth that You have not given me a spirit of fear but of power, love and self-control (2 Timothy 1:7). Please reveal to my mind now all the fears that have been controlling me so that I can renounce them and be free to walk by faith in You. I thank You for the freedom You give me to walk by faith and not by fear. In Jesus' powerful name I pray, Amen.

The following list may help you to recognize some of the fears that the devil has used to keep you from walking by faith. Check the ones that apply to your life. Write down any others that the Spirit of God brings to your mind. Then, one-by-one, renounce those fears aloud, using the suggested declaration on the next page.

____ Fear of death

____ Fear of Satan

____ Fear of failure

____ Fear of rejection by people

____ Fear of embarrassment

____ Fear of disapproval

____ Fear of being victimized

____ Fear of financial problems

____ Fear of marriage

____ Fear of never getting married

____ Fear of divorce

____ Fear of becoming homosexual

____ Fear of going crazy

____ Fear of the death of a loved one

____ Fear of pain

____ Fear of being a hopeless case

____ Fear of losing my salvation

____ Fear of not being loved by God

____ Fear of having committed the unpardonable sin

____ Fear of never being able to love or be loved by anyone

____ Other specific fears _____

I renounce the (name of the fear) because God has not given me a spirit of fear. I choose to live by faith in God, who has promised to protect me and meet all my needs as I walk by faith in Him (Psalm 27:1, Matthew 6:33-34).

After you have finished renouncing all the specific fears that you have allowed to control you, pray the following prayer from your heart:

❖ Dear Heavenly Father ❖

I thank You that You are trustworthy. I choose to believe You, even when my feelings and circumstances tell me to fear. You have told me not to fear, for You are with me; not to anxiously look about me, for You are my God. You will strengthen me, help me and surely uphold me with Your righteous right hand (Isaiah 41:10). I pray this with faith in the name of Jesus, Amen.

Analyze Your Fear

Knowing when and how you first experienced your fears is important in overcoming and living in victory. It is important when dealing with fear to have a responsible plan in place, so you will be ready to face any fears that come your way. Below are several questions that can help you in this area:

When did you first experience this fear, and what events preceded the first experience? What triggers this fear now?

What lies have you been believing about this fear?

How has this fear kept you from living a responsible life?

Note: For more help in this area of fear read *Freedom from Fear* by Neil Anderson or *Stomping Out Fear* by Neil T. Anderson and Dr. Dave Park. Visit infusionnow.org or call 865-966-1153 to order resources.

Overcoming Generational Sin

In the Lord's Prayer, Jesus wants you to claim and appropriate the spiritual protection that you have in Christ. It is important that you turn your back on the sins of your ancestors (parents, grandparents, great-grandparents, etc.) and any curses that may have been placed on you. Iniquities can be passed down from sinful members of one generation to the next (Exodus 20:4-6). You are not guilty of their sins, but Satan may have gained a foothold in your family because of these past sins. You must renounce any sins and curses of your ancestors and claim your spiritual freedom in Christ. In order to walk free from past influences, make the following declaration:

❖ Declaration ❖

I reject and disown all the sins of my ancestors, specifically _____. As one who has been delivered from the kingdom of darkness into the kingdom of God's dear Son, I cancel out all demonic working that has been passed on to me from my ancestors.

As one who has been crucified and raised with Jesus Christ and who sits with Him in heavenly places, I renounce all satanic assignments that are directed toward me, and I cancel every curse that Satan and his workers have put on me.

I announce to Satan and all his forces that Christ became a curse for me (Galatians 3:13) when He died for my sins on the cross. I reject any and every way in which Satan may claim ownership of me. I belong to the Lord Jesus Christ who purchased me with His own blood.

I reject all blood sacrifices whereby Satan may claim ownership of me. I declare myself to be eternally and completely signed over and committed to the Lord Jesus Christ. By the authority that I have in Jesus Christ, I now command every familiar spirit and every enemy of the Lord Jesus Christ that is in or around me to leave my presence. I commit myself to my heavenly Father, to do His will from this day forward.

The Armor of God

Using the prayer on the next page, take time now to pray on the armor of God. As believers, we are wise to do this each day and declare our total dependence on God. Remember, you are praying on real spiritual armor. You are putting on Christ Jesus (Romans 13:14)

I put on the belt of truth: Father, give me a hunger for Your word. I know that it is truth and I want my life to be centered in You and Your word. You have promised that the truth would set me free (John 8:32), so I put on the belt of truth and choose to believe the truth and speak the truth in love.

I put on the breastplate of righteousness: Father, I thank You that all the power of sin was canceled on the cross and that when I trusted in Jesus as my Savior, all my sins were washed away. Now I am righteous and holy in Your sight (Romans 5:1). You have made me completely acceptable to You. I am a saint, a holy one (Ephesians 1:1). I put on Your righteousness to help me walk in Your ways.

I put on the shoes of the gospel of peace: Father, I want to be ready for any spiritual battle and go wherever You want me to go. I choose to be salt and light for others on earth (Matthew 5:13-14). I choose to be Your witness for Christ (Acts 1:8).

I choose to be a minister of reconciliation and bring people and You back together (2 Corinthians 5:17-21). I choose to be an instrument of peace and choose to forgive, heal, restore, and bless those around me. I choose to live at peace with everyone (Ephesians 2:14, Philippians 4:13).

I take up the shield of faith: Father, I proclaim that Jesus is the only object of my faith (Galatians 2:20, Hebrews 13:8). I believe that You hear me and answer me when I call upon You. Thank You that You have given me all the faith I need to live for You today (Romans 12:3). I go forward now, putting out the fiery darts of fear, doubt, inadequacy, and unbelief, and proclaim that Jesus is my strength.

I put on the helmet of salvation: Father, I thank You for my salvation. Thank You for making me Your child and that You are my "Abba" Father. I thank you that no one can condemn me now that I am in Christ (Romans 8:1,31) and that nothing can separate me from You or Your love (Romans 8:35). Because of Your gift of salvation, I am sure that all things will work together for good (Romans 8:28). I claim all the victory of Jesus for my life as my Lord, Savior, Redeemer, and Deliverer. I have the mind of Christ and am complete in Him (Colossians 2:10).

I take up the sword of the Spirit, the spoken word of God: Father, You gave me Jesus, who is the Word of God living in me. I choose to be filled with Your Spirit and to obey You and Your word. Fill my mind (heart) with Your word so that in my time of need, I might recall to my mind Your truth. Lord, I take the offensive and use Your word as a spiritual weapon to destroy spiritual roadblocks and claim my victory in Christ (James 4:7). I choose this day to keep my eyes on Jesus and walk in step with the Spirit (John 1:1-4; 6:63) Amen.

"For Yours is the kingdom and the power and the glory forever, Amen"

Although this benediction is not included at the end of the Lord's Prayer in many manuscripts, it is fitting to end this time of prayer worshipping our Father. A benediction is a blessing. When you pray, "For Yours is the kingdom, and the power and the glory, forever," you are blessing God in three ways. First, you are blessing God by recognizing His kingdom and His sovereign right to rule over your life. You're announcing that He has the right to answer your prayers in His way, knowing He will do what is best for you. Second, by praying "power," you are proclaiming that God has the strength and ability to answer your prayers, and nothing in heaven or on earth can stop Him. Third, by praying "glory," you are giving God all the credit for your forgiveness, freedom, and blessings in your life.

Bless God now with the following benediction:

❖ Dear Heavenly Father ❖

I bless Your Holy Name for You have made me your child, purchased from sin by the blood of the Lord Jesus Christ. You are the Lord of the universe and the Lord of my life. You are my King, and I worship You alone. I submit my body to You as an instrument of righteousness, a living sacrifice, that I may glorify You in my body. I ask You to fill me now with Your Holy Spirit. I choose to live by Your Spirit's power. I commit myself to the renewing of my mind in order to prove that Your will is good, perfect, and acceptable for me (Romans 12:2). I will give You all the glory for my victory in Christ, for Yours is the kingdom, and the power and the glory, forever and ever, Amen.

A Few Words

Through this Prayer Journey, you have taken significant steps to bring yourself back into peace with God. You have applied the model for prayer that Jesus gave his disciples, not as a formula but as personal encounter with your Heavenly Father. You have allowed the Holy Spirit to guide you. Continue to live out your life in this prayerful attitude, seeking the revelation and the guidance of the Holy Spirit in your life. Come back to these petitions often. Be quick to worship your Father, seek His guidance, and yield to His plans. Do not rely on yourself for daily provision; rely on God. Claim the freedom and receive the forgiveness that the Father offers you in Jesus.

You may find influences attempting to reestablish the stronghold that was destroyed. One victory does not mean that the war is over. Freedom must be maintained. You will stay free as long as you remain in right relationship with God. If you should slip and fall, immediately get up and get right with God again.

Below are some suggestions of ways that help you maintain the intimacy and freedom you have experienced with your Abba Father today.

- ❖ Commit yourself to God's word. Make time daily to read the Bible. Let your thoughts dwell on God's truth and commit His words to your memory. Remember, when you come across a truth, believe it; a promise, claim it; a command, commit to obeying it!

- ❖ Devote yourself to prayer. Talk to your "Abba" Father regularly, frequently, all the time! Connect with Him by sharing your thoughts and feelings, but also by listening for His encouragement and prompts. Utilize the 6R approach discussed in message 3 of EPIC Freedom (page 57) to repent of any sin He reveals.

- ❖ Over each of the next 40 days, consider one of the "Who I am in Christ" statements (page 32-33 or 40-41), Read the associated scripture and claim this statement, out loud, as your identity (eg "I am a child of God;" "I am a saint")

- ❖ Take the next 40 days and work through *"Free,"* a devotional by Neil Anderson and Dave Park (https://bit.ly/FreeDevo), which will help you grow in your experience of identity and freedom in Christ and win the battle for the mind.

- ❖ Get involved in a church. Connect weekly with other Christians for worship and encouragement. Meet with a close friend or a small group of believers to share your struggles and victories. You must engage in Christian community to fully live out your identity and freedom in Christ!

For more information and resources check out our website at
infusionnow.org or call us at 865-966-1153.

Following Jesus to the Cross

Deny Yourself

> *"Then Jesus said to His disciples, 'If anyone wishes to come after Me, he must **deny** himself and **take up** his cross and **follow me**'"* (Matthew 16:24).

- It's not self-denial.

- You have to serve somebody (Matthew 6:24). We like to think that we can be our own masters. This is a delusion. The Bible tells us that we are either a slave to God or a slave to sin and Satan (John 8:34, Romans 6:11-18, 2 Timothy 2:25-26). Living according to the values of the ungodly world around us is the same as being a slave to Satan, for he is "the god of this world" (1 John 2:15-17; 5:9).

- Choose the new life of serving Christ (John 12:24-26, Galatians 2:20).

Take up your cross daily (Luke 9:23)

Every day we must remind ourselves that we are completely forgiven for all our sins through Christ's death on the cross (Colossians 2:13-14, Hebrews 10:10,17-18). Through Christ's death on the cross, we have also been set free from slavery to sin to live a new life for God (John 8:36). By the Spirit, we need to make the daily choice to put to death the deeds of our flesh (Romans 8:13).

Follow me

The decision to follow Christ is ours alone. No one can make that choice for us. The power to follow Christ, however, comes only from the Holy Spirit who lives inside us. If we are not led by the Spirit, we will soon get tired of resisting temptation and give in to sin (Galatians 5:16-17, 25, Romans 8:9-14).

> *"For whoever would save his life will lose it, but whoever loses his life for my sake will find it. For what will it profit a man if he gains the whole world and forfeits his soul? Or what shall a man give in return for his soul? For the Son of Man is going to come with his angels in the glory of his Father, and then he will repay each person according to what he has done"* (Matthew 16:25-27).

Finding Life and Joy in Christ (Matthew 16:25-27)

- Give up the low life to gain the higher (v. 25).

- Give up the pleasure of things to gain the pleasure of life (v. 26).

- Give up the things that are temporary to gain the eternal (v. 27).

Call to Ministry (Isaiah 6:1-8)

- Everyone has a ministry.

- Some are called to full-time vocational ministry.

- One call is not better than the other. (What does God want?)

If you've ever been presented with the thought that your gender is different from your biological sex, you're not alone. If you've ever heard a voice telling you that you might be genderless or gender fluid, you're not alone. You're not alone because the Lord Jesus Christ has also been tempted (tested) in the same way.

> *"For we do not have a high priest who is unable to sympathize with our weaknesses, but one who in* **every respect** *[emphasis added] has been tempted as we are, yet without sin. Let us then with confidence draw near to the throne of grace, that we may receive mercy and find grace to help in time of need"* (Hebrews 4:15-16).

Gender dysphoria is a conflict between a person's biological sex and his/her self-perceived gender identity. Maybe your battle with gender dysphoria has been confined to your thought life; maybe you have attempted to alleviate the tension by changing your appearance, taking hormonal medications, or undergoing surgery to bring your body more into alignment with your perceived gender. Whatever the case, if you have trusted in Jesus alone for the forgiveness of your sins, you are a new creation in Christ, and fully equipped to dismantle the stronghold of gender dysphoria. Today, as you fight this fight, He invites you to draw near to his throne of grace to receive mercy and find grace in your time of need.

Isaiah 42:3 says, *"a bruised reed he will not break, and a faintly burning wick he will not quench;"* His heart and intent toward you is to fan your soul into a flame of abundant life, not to snuff you out in your time of need.

Begin by praying this to the one who sees you, knows you, and relates to you and your struggles:

❖ Lord Jesus ❖

I believe that when you walked this earth you experienced every temptation possible, including the same temptations that harass me. You did not give in to these temptations but set an example for me of complete faithfulness to the Father. You are my high priest, through whom I receive mercy to help me in my time of need. Holy Spirit, today I set aside the agendas of the world, my own flesh and the devil. Speak to me and lead me into the light of your glorious truth and freedom. In Jesus' name I pray, Amen.

Affirm that Jesus is Your Creator

"For by him [Jesus] all things were created, in heaven and on earth, visible and invisible, whether thrones or dominions or rulers or authorities—all things were created through him and for him" (Colossians 1:16).

"In the beginning the Word already existed. The Word was with God, and the Word was God. He existed in the beginning with God. God created everything through him, and nothing was created except through him" (John 1:1-3 NLT).

Jesus, the perfect high priest who relates to everything you go through, is more than that – He is your creator! In concert with the will of the Father and the power of the Spirit, He created you wonderfully and uniquely for Himself and His purposes. He has meticulously fashioned your spirit, soul, body, gender, personality, skills, spiritual gifts, and He has declared that you are "very good" (Genesis 1:31). As your Creator, He alone has the right to define who you really are.

However, the effect of mankind's rebellion against the Creator is that everything in His created order broke and is in need of restoration (Romans 8:18-23). This means that there is not one aspect of our original design that has not been greatly distorted by sin (see EPIC Identity, Message 2, pp 16-20). Manifestations of this brokenness in human sexuality include: fornication (sexual relations outside of biblical marriage), infidelity, homosexuality, and gender confusion, to name a few. Unfortunately, another effect of the fall is that we are now tempted to look to ourselves, other people, lying spirits, and even our own brokenness for a sense of personal identity.

Honor Him today as your creator, acknowledge the brokenness of your life in need of restoration, and internalize the truth that only He has the right to define who you are. Pray this:

❖ Dear Lord Jesus ❖

You are my creator. You have made me to play an important and unique role in your big restoration project. I begin with my need for personal renovation - I desire to live more and more like the person that I already am in Christ. I withhold no part of my life from your healing, life-giving touch — not even how I feel about my sexual desires or gender identity. I agree that you alone have the right to define me, because you made me! In Jesus' name I pray, Amen.

Affirm that He is for you

"For one will scarcely die for a righteous person—though perhaps for a good person one would dare even to die— but God shows His love for us in that while we were still sinners, Christ died for us" (Romans 5:7-8).

"For I know the plans I have for you, declares the LORD, plans for welfare and not for evil, to give you a future and a hope" (Jeremiah 29:11).

Your own sense of gender identity does not define who you are – the cross of Christ defines who you are: a precious child of God who is loved, accepted and eternally blessed by Him. Romans 5:7-8 teaches that because God has already loved you when you were a sinner at your lowest and worst, He will continue to love you unconditionally.

Jesus has purchased you spirit, soul and body, and He cares more for your well-being and future than you, or anyone else does! On the basis of His sacrificial love, He has proven that He is the only worthy object of your trust. You can rely on Him to speak to you through his word and Spirit. Even through the pain of gender confusion, He leads you in a way that results in your highest good, the good of others, and his glory. Affirm your conviction that this is true:

❖ Heavenly Father ❖

Thank you for your unconditional and steadfast love. Because you sent your son to pay the penalty my sins deserved, I know I am loved. Lord Jesus, because you placed my well-being above your own, I trust what you say more than I trust the lies of the enemy or my own thoughts, feelings and emotions. Holy Spirit, because I have received Christ, I rejoice that you have come to dwell within me, strengthening me to do your will. Now I lay my will down before your amazing love and grace. Jesus, as my Creator and Savior you've more than earned the right to direct my life, for your glory and my highest good. In Jesus' name I pray, Amen.

Affirm that God and his word are supreme

Consider closely these scriptures:

"For my thoughts are not your thoughts, neither are your ways my ways,declares the LORD. For as the heavens are higher than the earth, so are my ways higher than your ways and my thoughts than your thoughts" (Isaiah 55:8-9).

All Scripture is breathed out by God and profitable for teaching, for reproof, for correction, and for training in righteousness, that the man of God may be complete, equipped for every good work. (2 Timothy 3:16-17).

"Trust in the LORD with all your heart, and do not lean on your own understanding. In all your ways acknowledge him, and he will make straight your paths" (Proverbs 3:5-6).

As recorded in John 17:16-17, Jesus prayed this to the Father on behalf of all his disciples (including you): "*They are not of the world, just as I am not of the world. Sanctify them in the truth; your word is truth.*" To tear down the spiritual stronghold of gender dysphoria, God asks no more of you than He asks of anyone else dealing with a temptation that seems impossible to resist — set aside your own thoughts, understanding and feelings to trust in his perfect knowledge, transforming love, and absolute authority.

God declares that the distance between our thoughts and ways compared to His is comparable to the distance between the ground under our feet and the furthest star in the universe. Given that the closest star to us, the sun, is 93 million miles away, that's a breathtaking contrast!

The point is this – He who created all things has revealed His higher will and ways to us through His word. In Christ, the Holy Spirit opens our minds to the authority of the scriptures. His word is indeed truth. Thoughts and feelings about gender, or anything else, do not dictate what is true – His word dictates what is true. This is critically important, because other voices (some well-meaning) continually threaten to drown out God's voice in our lives. Take a moment and ask the Holy Spirit to reveal which voices you have given more weight to than God's voice, especially in this question of gender identity.

_____ Satan and his demons

_____ family and friends

_____ popular culture, including movies, TV shows, videos, podcasts, vlogs & radio programs

_____ doctors, psychiatrists and social scientists

_____ social media

_____ celebrities

_____ politicians

_____ influential professional and social organizations

_____ the flesh (that remnant of your pre-Christ life that influences us to meet our needs apart from Him).

Now, pray the following:

❖ Almighty God ❖

All wisdom belongs to you, and you alone are the creator and rightful ruler of the universe. Your voice and will are supreme. Your word expressed through the Holy Bible is true and authoritative. In this area of gender identity, I confess that I have listened to and believed these voices above your voice (be specific): _____

I renounce allegiance to any other voice (human or spirit) telling me what is contrary to your will and ways. In your name, Jesus, I command any spiritual forces of evil to be silenced and leave my presence. Father, I gladly receive your forgiveness and affirm as Jesus did: I do not live by bread alone, but by every word that comes from your mouth. I delight myself in you. Holy Spirit, create within me new thoughts, feelings, desires, and dreams consistent with the Father's will for me (Psalm 37:4). You have my listening ear, my responsive heart, and my willing obedience. In Jesus' name I pray, Amen.

Come Home

In the parable of the prodigal son (Luke 15:11-32), Jesus makes clear how we are to respond when temptations lead us to stray from the one who has passionately loved us and adopted us as his children (Ephesians 1:5, John 1:12). He simply calls us to come home! This is a beautiful picture of what scripture calls "repentance." Repentance is a 180-degree change of mind, resulting in a 180-degree change of choices, words and actions. The result is restored fellowship with God, a renewed mind, transformation and joy!

Now consider what Jesus, the Creator and Savior, says with respect to gender identity:

"...from the beginning of creation, 'God made them male and female. Therefore a man shall leave his father and mother and hold fast to his wife, and the two shall become one flesh.' So they are no longer two but one flesh. What therefore God has joined together, let not man separate" (Mark 10:6-9).

"So God created man in his own image, In the image of God he created him; Male and female he created them" (Genesis 1:26).

From these scriptures, what do we learn about God's original design with respect to gender?

First, God has created the human race in a strictly binary fashion, meaning there are only two genders, male and female.

Second, God's decree that "the two shall become one...they are no longer two but one flesh" means that male and female are created distinctly to complement each other — to fit each other physically, emotionally and spiritually. He created woman to be a helper, custom made for man (Genesis 2:18), and his partner in bearing children, filling the earth, and subduing it (Genesis 1:28). God has clearly communicated that each gender is distinct and not interchangeable with the other.

Third, as the sole creator of every person, Jesus has wonderfully created you with your unique physical features, personality, and talents. He has also "assigned" your gender as male or female. The whole of scripture affirms that God has created humanity so that there is a unity between biological sex and gender identity. Your gender at conception, evidenced by your biology at birth, is your true God-given gender, and is a precious gift to be used for God's glory.

1 Corinthians 6:19-20 declares: "...*do you not know that your body is a temple of the Holy Spirit within you, whom you have from God? You are not your own, for you were bought with a price. So glorify God in your body.*"

This scripture signifies that none of us has the right to do whatever we want with our bodies. At the cross, Jesus purchased us, inside out, and from head to toe. Our bodies are his, to direct as He pleases.

The scriptures speak of behaviors to confess and renounce, because they are at odds with your God-given gender:

- A man must not behave sexually as a woman; a woman must not behave sexually as a man (Leviticus 18:22, Romans 1:18-32, 1 Corinthians 6:9-10).

- A woman must not dress in order to present herself as a man; a man must not dress himself in order to present himself as a woman (Deuteronomy 22:5).

These commands encompass other measures you may have taken, or been tempted to take, in order to identify with the opposite sex (check or list any activity the Holy Spirit brings to mind):

_____ Changing my hairstyle

_____ Packing (when a woman takes measures to appear to have male genitalia)

_____ Tucking (when a man takes measures to appear not to have male genitalia)

_____ Binding (when a woman takes measures to de-accentuate her breasts to appear as a man)

_____ Augmenting my figure (when a man places inserts into his clothing to simulate a more feminine figure)

_____ Hormone therapy

_____ Surgeries to my face, chest or genitals

_____ Hair removal from my face or body (making a man appear more feminine)

_____ Speech therapy, so I sound more like someone of the opposite sex

_____ "Coming out" to my family, friends and others by presenting myself as the opposite of my God-given gender

_____ Making changes to my legal documents to express a change of gender, name, and preferred pronouns

_____ Other_____

Now, God invites and calls you to "come home" (repent) and pray:

❖ Dear Jesus ❖

your Spirit has graciously revealed to me that I have elevated my feelings, beliefs and actions above your word. My feelings do not make lies true. I have wandered from you, but now I come home to your loving arms. I repent of believing that my gender identity is different from the one you created me with. I also repent specifically of these actions I have considered or taken (items you checked above):_____ .
Now, I gladly receive your forgiveness, because you have promised to forgive me (1 John 1:9). I renew my mind by declaring that I am a new creation in Christ. I am a child of God, and a saint! I also agree with you, my creator, high priest, and savior, that you have made me _____ (male/female). I resist and command any voice opposed to this truth to be silenced, in Jesus' name!

I now commit, with your Spirit's power, and the help of my brothers and sisters in Christ, to think and act in accordance with my real gender. In Jesus' name I pray, Amen.

Forgive

Forgiveness is like TNT in tearing down spiritual strongholds! Be sure to forgive those who have:

- abused you verbally, physically or sexually. These abuses are common delivery vehicles for lies about gender and sexuality. Renounce any lies the Spirit reveals that were ushered in through instances of abuse.

- influenced you, directly or indirectly, towards transgenderism as a means of trying to alleviate your gender confusion.

- mocked or persecuted you in your expressions of gender identity. This includes those who have either called into question your God-given gender, or who have ridiculed you, as you have acted in ways contrary to your God-given gender.

* Revisit Petition 7 (pg. 106) in this prayer journey, as needed.

Going Forward

As you grapple with how God's truth differs from what you have thought and felt, it is important to understand that being tempted to sin is not the same thing as engaging in sin. When you are confronted with voices calling your gender identity into question, you are not sinning. Whenever this happens, take the thought captive immediately, renounce it, and use your authority in Christ to silence the lying voice of the enemy. Then, counter the lie with God's truth.

In many cases, generational sin must be addressed. We all live under the influence of our ancestors, including tendencies toward certain patterns of sin (Exodus 20:5-6). While gender confusion may or may not be a part of your family's history, there may be patterns of sexual sin, including abuse, that have opened doors to the enemy's influence concerning your gender. As observation or revelation by the Holy Spirit reveals sin patterns from your family history, you have the right and the obligation to confess the sins of your family line, along with your own contributions to intergenerational sin (see Nehemiah 1:6; 9:1-2).

* See Overcoming Generational Sin in Petition 9 (pg. 119) for help with this.

Be sure to pray for and seek out believers who will love you just as you are, and walk the path of restoration with you, faithfully pointing you to your true identity and freedom in Christ.

Over time (or instantly, in some cases) the Lord may remove all thoughts and feelings associated with gender dysphoria from your life. However, even if these persist, He will strengthen you by His grace to desire and act according His will, rather than according to your feelings.

Remember, Jesus has indeed been tempted in every way, including being exposed to lies about gender identity. However, He never gave in to this temptation by denying the Father's gender assignment for Him. He invites you to follow closely in His wake, be strengthened by His grace, and enjoy fullness of life with Him. He is not in the business of ruining your life, but in fulfilling your life now and eternally.

Conclude this time by praying according to the spirit of Romans 12:1-2:

❖ Dear Father ❖

I give you my mind and body because of all you have done for me. Let them be a living and holy sacrifice to you— for this is the kind of worship you find acceptable. I will not copy the behavior and customs of this world. Instead, I will let you transform me fully into the new person I already am, by changing the way I think, speak and act. In this way, I will learn to know and do your will for me, which is good and pleasing and perfect. In Jesus' wonderful and powerful name, Amen.

40 Predictive Prophecies

Prophecy	Old Testament Prediction	New Testament Fulfillment
1 Born of a woman	Genesis 3:15	Galatians 4:4
2 Descendant of Abraham	Genesis 12:1-3	Matthew 1:1
3 Descendant of Isaac	Genesis 17:19	Luke 3:34
4 Descendant of Jacob	Numbers 24:17	Matthew 1:2
5 From the tribe of Judah	Genesis 49:10	Luke 3:32-32
6 Of the house of David	2 Samuel 7:12	Matthew 1:1
7 Heir to the throne of David	Isaiah 9:7	Luke 1:32-33
8 He would be born in Bethlehem	Micah 5:2	Luke 2:4-7
9 Anointed by the Holy Spirit	Isaiah 11:2	Matthew 3:16-17
10 Born of a virgin	Isaiah 7:14	Luke 1:26-27, 30-31
11 Time of His birth	Daniel 9:24-25	483 years after 444 B.C.
12 Heralded by a messenger	Isaiah 40:3	Luke 3:3-6
13 Preceded by a forerunner	Malachi 3:1	Luke 7:24, 27

Prophecy	Old Testament Prediction	New Testament Fulfillment
14 Preceded by Elijah	Malachi 4:5-6	Matthew 11:13-14
15 Ministry of miracles	Isaiah 35:5	Matthew 9:35
16 He will cleanse the temple	Malachi 3:1	Matthew 21:12
17 Rejected by His Jewish people	Psalm 118:22	1 Peter 2:7
18 Declared the Son of God	Psalm 2:7	Matthew 3:17
19 He will minister in Galilee	Isaiah 9:1	Matthew 4:13-16
20 He will speak in parables	Psalm 78:2-4	Matthew 13:34-35
21 Triumphal entry	Zechariah 9:9	Mark 11:7, 9, 11
22 He will die a humiliating death	Psalm 22	Matthew 27
23 Betrayed by a close friend	Psalm 41:9	Luke 22:47-48
24 Betrayed for thirty pieces of silver	Zechariah 11:12	Matthew 26:15
25 Accused by false witness	Psalm 35:11	Mark 14:57
26 Silent before accusers	Isaiah 53:3, 7	Matthew 27:12-19
27 He will be sneered and mocked	Psalm 22:7	Luke 23:35

Prophecy	Old Testament Prediction	New Testament Fulfillment
28 He will be spat on and struck	Isaiah 50:6	Matthew 26:67
29 Piercing His hands and feet	Psalm 22:16	Luke 23:33
30 Being crucified with thieves	Isaiah 53:12	Matthew 17:38
31 Pray for His enemies	Psalm 109:4, Isaiah 53:12	Luke 23:34
32 Thirst on the cross	Psalm 69:21	John 19:28
33 Gambled for His clothes	Psalm 22:17-18	John 19:23
34 Forsaken by God	Psalm 22:1	Matthew 27:46
35 No bones broken	Psalm 34:20	John 19:32-33, 36
36 His side pierced	Zechariah 12:10	John 19:34
37 Buried in a rich man's tomb	Isaiah 53:9	Matthew 27:57-60
38 He will be resurrected	Psalm 2:7; 16:10; 49:15	Mark 16:6,7, Acts 2:31
39 He will ascend into heaven	Psalm 68:18	Acts 1:9
40 He will sit at the right hand of God	Psalm 110:1	Hebrews 1:3

Bibliographical Evidence—Number of Manuscripts

Only a divine being can make these kinds of precise predictions, even some four or even six hundred years before they happened. When so many of these prophecies converge in the lifetime of one man, it becomes nothing less than miraculous.

Can we trust our Bible? Are there enough early manuscripts of the New Testament or Old Testament to conclude that it has been accurately transmitted? The New Testament far exceeds any other historical document in this category. *There are over 24,000 early manuscripts or manuscript fragments, including more than 5,300 in the original Greek language.* There are complete collections of the New Testament books preserved in a bound fashion similar to today's Bible. We call these codices. Compare this with only 193 copies of the writings of Sophocles, and it is clear that the preservation of the New Testament manuscripts is awesome. We have the same New Testament letters in our hands today that the early church had, they match perfectly!

Did you know that of all documents prior to the second century, The Iliad by Homer comes in a distant second with only 643 manuscript fragments. No one doubts that we are reading The Iliad as Homer wrote it because we have so many copies, yet the New Testament has over 24,000, and we question the Bible. Amazing, isn't it? We can trust our Bible!

Accuracy of Manuscripts

When compared to each other, how accurate do these manuscripts appear? Do they all say the same thing? Naturally, the more manuscripts available, the less likely they would be to match precisely.

The Bible defies these odds. While there are not enough copies to determine the accuracy of most historical documents, the New Testament is generally regarded as 99+% accurate. The small percentage of inaccuracies is usually insignificant spelling and/or wording changes. There are virtually no changes in significant meaning.

One of the great evidences of this occurred with the discovery of the Dead Sea Scrolls and actually applies to the Old Testament documents. Prior to this discovery, the oldest known Hebrew manuscript of the entire Bible was the Aleppo Codex, written about 900 AD. When the scrolls were unearthed, scholars were amazed to find the text to be virtually identical to the Aleppo Codex, despite the fact that they dated about 200 BC - over 1000 years earlier!

Period of Time Elapsed

How much time elapsed between the original writing and the earliest copy we have available today? A longer time span from the original would mean more generations of copies, thus more room for human error. Most of the early copies we have of New Testament documents date to within 90 years of the original; some may be closer than 20 years. Until recently, a fragment of the Gospel of John, dated about 125 AD, was the earliest known copy of any part of the New Testament. In 1972, however, nine New Testament manuscript fragments were found in the caves near the Dead Sea. Among these were part of Mark dated about 50 AD, part of Luke dated about 57 AD and part of Acts from 66 AD. Remarkably, this places these copies not more than a decade or two (and perhaps only a few years) from the original documents.

Complete New Testament manuscripts have been found, such as *Codex Vaticanus* and *Codex Sinaiticus*, which are dated to 325-50 AD and 350 AD, respectively. Compare this to the earliest copies of Sophocles' writings dated 1,400 years after the original.

Comparison to Other Literary Works

The following table shows how other historical, literary works compare to the Bible. First, note the number of extant copies (copies made from the original) still in existence. Also, note how narrow the time span is between the original and the earliest copies. Of the two major steps involved in textual criticism, no other literary work in history can compare to the Bible. (Information condensed and adapted from Josh McDowell, *Evidence That Demands A Verdict,* Here's Life Publishers, Inc., San Bernardino, CA, 1992, pp. 42-43.)

> There is simply no other book that is as textually accurate as the Bible, nothing even close.
> God knew we needed His Word and He preserved and protected it for us.
> We can trust God's Word!

Comparisons of other Literary Works Table

Work/Author	Date written	Earliest copy	Years elapsed	Number of copies
Caesar	100-44 BC	900 AD	1,000	10
Plato	427-347 BC	900 AD	1,200	7
Sophocles	496-406 BC	1000 AD	1,400	193
Aristotle	384-322 BC	1100 AD	1,400	49
Iliad (Homer)	900 BC	400 BC	500	643
Tacitus	100 AD	1100 AD	1,000	20
Thucydides	460-400 BC	900 AD	1,300	8
Herodotus	480-425 BC	900 AD	1,300	8
Euripedes	480-406 BC	1100 AD	1,500	9
Aristophanes	450-385 BC	900 AD	1,200	10
New Testament	**40-90 AD**	**50 AD**	**< 20**	**24,000**

Jesus Really Lived

There is an extensive body of evidence to support the existence of Christ. Both the excellent historical text of the New Testament and numerous secular historians record the events of His life. Numerous early writers reference Christ, including Thallus, Suetonius, Phlegon (known only by references from Origen), Pliny the younger, Origen, and the Jewish Talmud. In Origen's document *Against Celsus*, he writes:

"And with regard to the eclipse in the time of Tiberius Caesar, in whose reign Jesus appears to have been crucified, and the great earthquakes which then took place, Phlegon too, I think, has written in the thirteenth or fourteenth book of his Chronicles." (Origen. Against Celsus 2.33, from Roberts, Alexander, and Donaldson, James, eds. The Ante-Nicene Fathers. Grand Rapids: William B. Eerdsmans Publishing Co., 1973.)

Origen clearly identifies Jesus as a known man during the time of Tiberius Caesar. Another popular reference is that of Josephus, a Jewish historian born just a few years after Jesus died. In his book, *The Antiquities of the Jews* finished in 93 A.D. Josephus writes:

"About this time there lived Jesus, a wise man, if indeed one ought to call him a man. For he was one who wrought surprising feats and was a teacher of such people as accepted the truth gladly. He won over many Jews and many of the Greeks. He was the Messiah. When Pilate, upon hearing him accused by men of the highest standing amongst us, had condemned him to be crucified, those who had in the first place come to love him did not give up their affection for him. On the third day he appeared to them restored to life, for the prophets of God had prophesied these and countless other marvelous things about him. And the tribe of the Christians, so called after him, has still to this day not disappeared."

Jesus Claimed to be God, the Messiah

Regarding His claim of deity, it is well substantiated. It was thought to be heretical by the Jews and was precisely why they wanted Him dead. Check out the following passages:

"The woman said,' know that Messiah (called Christ) is coming. When he comes, he will explain everything to us.' Then Jesus declared, 'I, the one speaking to you—I am he'" John 4:25-26).

"Jesus said to her, 'I am the resurrection and the life. The one who believes in me will live, even though they die; and whoever lives by believing in me will never die. Do you believe this?' 'Yes, Lord,' she replied, 'I believe that you are the Messiah, the Son of God, who is to come into the world'" (John 11:25-27) .

The life of Christ is a matter of historical fact

As F.F. Bruce points out,

"Some writers may toy with the fancy of a 'Christ-myth,' but they do not do so on the ground of historical evidence. The historicity of Christ is as axiomatic for an unbiased historian as the historicity of Julius Caesar. It is not historians who propagate the 'Christ-myth' theories."

(Bruce, F.F. *The New Testament Documents*. 5th Ed. Grand Rapids: William B. Eerdsmans Publishing Co., p.119.)

Jesus suffered, was crucified and gave up His life

- Christ was stripped and bound to a column.
- Christ was whipped with a rod or flexible reed.

> Christ was scourged with a whip: The whip was made of broken pottery, lead balls and bone chips. He was beaten by two men alternating their blows. His shoulders, loins, thighs and calves were beaten. Christ's skin was already sore from sweating drops of blood. Long blue bruises begin to form and the lead balls begin to tear away strips of Christ's skin. Christ lost tremendous amounts of blood and became weak. Christ never opened His mouth. His bound wrists prevented Him from slumping to the bloody stone ground. The executioners stopped short of killing Christ only because they were commanded not to kill Him.

- Christ was given a purple legionnaires cape, a mocking symbol of His royalty.
- Christ was given a crown of two and a half inch Judean thorns; it was thrust down on His head.
- Christ was mocked, and they beat Him, slapped Him, and spat on Him while calling Him the "King of the Jews."
- Christ was taken to Pilate and the crowd of people cried, "Crucify Him!"
- Christ's purple cloak was now dried on His back from the coagulated blood. They ripped it off of Him, opening all the wounds which caused more blood to flow.
- Christ was given a cross weighing approximately 125 pounds.
- Christ, barefoot and bound, now traveled some 650 yards uphill to the place of the skull. The Romans pulled His cords, wondering if He would die before they reached the mountain top.
- Christ's back, again, began to bleed as the cross scraped and stripped open His wounds.

It's true that Jesus endured six trials, a crown of thorns, Roman scourging, and finally, His hands and feet were pierced as He was nailed to the cross. A spear was thrust into His side, and ultimately He was pronounced dead by a centurion—but let's take a more detailed look at the death of Christ:

- Christ was so weak that Simon of Cyrene was finally asked to carry the cross.
- He was laid on His back; His wounds were caked with dust and fine gravel.
- Christ, with His shoulder on the crosspiece, had His hand stretched over to the far end of the beam, where the executioner took a long square nail and nailed it through the forward fold of the hand.
- Christ's other hand was nailed to the other end of the beam.
- Christ was still silent as His thumbs struck the center of His palms because the median nerve had been touched. This sent continual shock waves to His brain whenever He moved and was in excruciating pain.
- Christ was then lifted some seven feet in the air by His hands to the vertical crossbar.
- Christ's knees were bent, with His left foot placed against the rough timber as another square nail was driven through the second or third metatarsal.
- Christ's right foot was placed over the left, and a second nail traveled through both feet, locking them together.
- Christ was offered an anesthetic of gall and wine, but He didn't accept it.
- Christ's body began to cramp as every muscle tightened.
- Christ's lungs had air, but as if He was an acute asthmatic, His face turned pale, purple and blue. He was asphyxiating; His lungs were full of air, but He was unable to release it.
- Christ had to lift Himself up onto His feet while the two nails supported His weight, to release the air trapped in His lungs.
- Christ did not even resemble a man, as swarms of flies cover the massive wounds all over His body.

- Christ experienced the worst torment of all while He was completely separated from the Father; their intimate fellowship was broken. The sky turned completely black and a deep darkness fell over all the earth. The earth began to shake as a massive earthquake struck the region. The graves were open and people who had died were resurrected and roamed the earth.

- "About the ninth hour Jesus cried out in a loud voice, saying, '*Eli, Eli, lema sabachthani?' (which means 'My God, my God, why have you forsaken me'")* (Matthew 27:46).

- Yet all this did not kill Christ, but rather He surrendered His life, saying, "'*Father, into your hands I commit my spirit'"* (Luke 23:46) .

- Jesus' head slumped forward, and the Son of God was dead.

The Romans would have first made sure that Christ was really dead and not just unconscious. They thrust a spear into His side, as they did many victims, to confirm that He was dead. If Jesus had not been dead, then they would have broken His legs, making it impossible for Him to move up and down on the cross and take in any air in His lungs. He would have quickly died from a lack of oxygen. This is what happened to the two men who were crucified with Christ.

- Jesus was speared in His side just under the breastbone, piercing the pericardial sack of His heart. Water and blood flowed out. The presence of water provided medical proof that Jesus was, in fact, dead as water is only present in the heart when a person is clinically dead. Jesus' legs were not broken because the executioner knew He was dead.

Jesus and the Tomb

Jesus was wrapped in 100 pounds of spices and placed in a tomb sealed with a large stone and Roman seal.

"When it was evening, there came a rich man from Arimathea, named Joseph, who also was a disciple of Jesus. He went to Pilate and asked for the body of Jesus. Then Pilate ordered it to be given to him. And Joseph took the body and wrapped it in a clean linen shroud and laid it in his own new tomb, which he had cut in the rock. And he rolled a great stone to the entrance of the tomb and went away" (Matthew 27:57-60).

Sealed and Guarded

The Jews were concerned about someone taking Christ's body, so they went to Pilate to commission Roman guards to watch the tomb.

"The next day, that is, after the day of Preparation, the chief priests and the Pharisees gathered before Pilate and said, 'Sir, we remember how that impostor said, while he was still alive, 'After three days I will rise.' Therefore order the tomb to be made secure until the third day, lest his disciples go and steal him away and tell the people, 'He has risen from the dead,' and the last fraud will be worse than the first.' Pilate said to them, 'You have a guard of soldiers. Go, make it as secure as you can.' So they went and made the tomb secure by sealing the stone and setting a guard" (Matthew 27:62-66).

Some have speculated as many as sixteen soldiers were at the tomb, as this was normally a minimum Roman fighting unit. This assertion is challenged on the basis that this was not a battle being waged. On the other hand, Roman law was at stake.

As Matthew indicates above, the guards set a seal on the stone. According to Roman custom, this was a seal of soft clay, usually over straps that spanned the stone itself. If the stone were moved, the straps and the seal would be broken. The seal itself would bear the mark of Caesar and indicate its placement by the highest authority in the land. The purpose of the setting a seal on the stone was not to literally lock it in place but to warn would-be intruders that breaking the seal was a violation of Roman law. Hence the Roman guards were there to enforce it. Archaeological discoveries dating back to the time of Christ have confirmed that the crime of grave robbing was punishable by death.

The Empty Tomb

The fact that the Jewish leaders bribed the guards to say the body was stolen implies that the body was missing. The tomb was empty, and the guards were looking for a way out so they wouldn't get punished for letting the body of Christ get away from them. Who moved the stone? We tend to overlook this point, yet placing ourselves at the scene, seeing the stone moved so far away from the tomb must have been amazing.

We know from the text that the size of the stone was big, really big! According to Mark 16:1-2, there were at least three women who knew they could not move it—even though it could be rolled—because it was *extremely large*. How much did it weigh? We don't know exactly, but it was likely near 1 ½ tons or more.

Would not the soldiers have heard such a massive object being moved if they were asleep? Would a weakened Jesus, beaten and stabbed, be able to summon the strength to move it?

The position of the stone after its movement was even more interesting. Matthew, Mark, and Luke use the Greek word "*apokulio*"— meaning to *roll away*—to describe the movement of the stone. This word would indicate that the stone had been rolled away from the opening, not *slightly moved*. John, however, is a little more specific.

In John 20:1, he uses the word "*airo*"—meaning *to pick up and carry away*—to describe the movement of the stone. This heavy rock was not moved slightly back from the opening but rather relocated away from the opening.

Considering that 108 cubic inches of granite weighs about 15 pounds (7.2ci per pound), we can easily estimate the weight. The size of the opening was low enough that the disciples had to stoop down, but big enough to easily get the body in—probably about three feet. Allowing for the stone to overlap the opening by six inches on each side, it then measures 48 inches across, or a 24-inch radius. It must have also been thick enough so as not to tip over—a minimum of 12 inches, perhaps more. The formula for calculating volume would then be $\pi r2w$—in this case, 21,715 cubic inches. Using the weight factor above (7.2), we can see that the stone probably weighed more than 3,000 pounds.

The Eye Witnesses

There were many sightings of Christ after His death. In one case, cited by Paul, He appeared to more than 500 people. Other cases recorded in the New Testament are:

Mary and Mary Magdalene	Matthew 28:9
The Eleven in Galilee	Matthew 28:16-17
Mary Magdalene	Mark 16:9
Two disciples (Road to Emmaus)	Luke 24:15-31
Ten apostles (without Thomas)	John 20:19,24
Eleven apostles	John 20:26-28
Seven disciples fishing	John 21:1-24
Eleven apostles	Acts 1:2-6
Peter	1 Corinthians 15:5
James	1 Corinthians 15:7
Paul	1 Corinthians 15:8
The five hundred	1 Corinthians 15:6

The secular Jewish historian, Josephus, confirms the apparent resurrection of Jesus, saying, **"On the third day he appeared to them restored to life..."**
(*Josephus, Antiquities of the Jews,* Loeb edition, vol. IX, 18.3.3. Translated by Lewis H. Feldman. Cambridge, MA: Harvard University Press, 1965.)

Collectively, the New Testament and other historical documents clearly indicate that many people sighted Jesus over a period of forty days after His death. He was seen in many different environments and activities indoors, outdoors, sitting, standing, walking, talking and eating.

Would you die for a lie?

You might die for a lie if you thought it was true, but you wouldn't die for something you were certain was a lie. Terrorists will die for a lie because they believe it's true. If the disciples knew that Jesus was really dead and had in fact not resurrected, they would not have given their lives to tell the world that He had risen. Peter was crucified. Andrew was crucified. Matthew was crucified. James, the son of Alphaeus, was crucified. Phillip was crucified. Simeon was crucified. Thaddeus was killed with arrows. James, the brother of Jesus, was stoned. Thomas was killed by a spear. Bartholomew was crucified. James, the son of Zebedee, was killed by the sword. Paul, the apostle, was beheaded with a sword. John was the only one who died of natural causes.

"Put on the whole armor of God, that you may be able to stand against the schemes of the devil. For we do not wrestle against flesh and blood, but against the rulers, against the authorities, against the cosmic powers over this present darkness, against the spiritual forces of evil in the heavenly places" (Ephesians 6:11-12).

Be prepared for ministry – put on the Armor of God

1. *Buckle up with the Belt of Truth*

- Fill your mind with the truth (John 8:31-32; 17:15-17).

- Speak the truth to others (Ephesians 4:15,25).

- The belt of truth protects you from the lies and deception of Satan (John 8:44, Revelation 12:9).

2. *Put on the Breastplate of Righteousness*

- In Christ, you are right with God (Romans 4:5, 1 Corinthians 1:30).

- If you sin, confess it right away (1 John 1:9-22).

- Live your life for Christ, not for sin (Romans 13:12-14).

- The breastplate of righteousness protects you from accusations and temptations (Revelation 12:10, Matthew 4:3).

3. *Stand firm and move out with the Sandals of the Gospel of Peace*

- Remember that you are already at peace with God (Romans 5:1).

- Don't worry, but let peace rule in your heart (Colossians 3:15, Philippians 4: 6-7).

- Share God's message of peace by your life and words (Matthew 5:9, 2 Corinthians 5:18-20).

- The sandals of the gospel of peace enable you to stand firm in the face of fear, anxiety, and persecution.

4. *Take up the Shield of Faith*

Knowing who God is, who you are in Christ and what the truth is, will enable you to walk in faith even when Satan fires his most painful arrows at you! Some of his flaming arrows are listed below:

Doubt	Guilt	Persecution	Fear
Loneliness	Gossip	Illness	Abuse
Anxiety	Discouragement/Depression		

Your faith can snuff out every fiery arrow that the devil shoots at you!

5. *Take the Helmet of Salvation*

- The helmet protects the most important part of your body, the head. Your mind is the place where spiritual battles are won or lost.

- The assurance of salvation is a key part of our spiritual armor. Those under attack by the devil very often have doubts about their salvation (1 John 5:11-13, John 10:27-30, 1 Thessalonians 5:8).

6. *Take up the Sword of the Spirit—the spoken Word of God*

- Satan can't read our minds so he doesn't have to obey our thoughts.

- Jesus, when He was tempted, spoke the Word of God aloud to Satan (Matthew 4:1-11). Satan was forced to leave Jesus.

- Satan is not impressed by our great arguments, loud voices, or strong personalities, however he must flee from the truth spoken by a Christian who is truly walking with God (James 4:7).

"Therefore take up the whole armor of God, that you may be able to withstand in the evil day, and having done all, to stand firm. Stand therefore, having fastened on the belt of truth, and having put on the breastplate of righteousness, and, as shoes for your feet, having put on the readiness given by the gospel of peace. In all circumstances take up the shield of faith, with which you can extinguish all the flaming darts of the evil one; and take the helmet of salvation, and the sword of the Spirit, which is the word of God" (Ephesians 6:13-17).

EPIC Events

Our passion at Infusion Ministries is to train pastors and other leaders to help their people understand what it means to be a child of God and walk in freedom from destructive habits. We provide training and resources for all ages and groups. In addition to the summits below, we have training tailored to parents, small group leaders and others. Contact us for more details and how you can join us in Knoxville, TN, for a summit, or bring these powerful truths to your church or ministry. Call (865) 966-1153, or visit infusionnow.org for the most up to date information on our events.

EPIC Summit

This three-day summit is held live in Knoxville, TN, and broadcast on ZOOM in the spring and fall, and consists of three parts:

- **Identity:** EPIC Identity material walks us through the biblical truths about who we are in Christ and how to replace the negative, false ideas we have believed about ourselves with these truths.
- **Freedom**: Satan wants to keep us in bondage to destructive habits, addictions, fear, anger, unforgiveness and more. But Jesus came to set us free. EPIC Freedom provides tools to win the battle for the mind and live in His freedom.
- **The Lord's Prayer Journey**: We utilize the Lord's Prayer as a means for the Holy Spirit to reveal any doors opened to the enemy, unresolved spiritual conflict or unforgiveness and help us claim freedom.

EPIC Leadership Summits

This two-day summit is held in Knoxville, TN, once a year.

- **EPIC Leader I**: So many leaders do not feel qualified or equipped to help those with spiritual conflicts and bondage. EPIC Leader I provides Biblical tools and principles that will help you bring the message of identity and freedom in Christ to your church or organization.
- **EPIC Leader II**: Provides material that will give you a clear model and guide to discipleship counseling and tools to help all believers overcome their spiritual conflicts.

EPIC Latino Summit

This is a five-day summit, held in Knoxville, TN, once a year in late summer.
EPIC Identity, Freedom and Journey are combined with EPIC Leadership 1
And Leadership 2 materials - all presented in Spanish. Contact us for information on the next EPIC Latino Summit.

The Holy Land Tour, led by Dr. Dave Park

During this life-altering journey, usually in June, we tour numerous natural, civic and religious sites described in scriptures and share in meaningful times of worship, instruction, and prayer. To find out more information about the next trip, visit our website at infusionnow.org.

Made in the USA
Monee, IL
15 April 2022

94794172R00083